BASKETBALL
SHORTS

BASKETBALL SHORTS

1,001 OF THE GAME'S FUNNIEST ONE-LINERS

GLENN LIEBMAN

CONTEMPORARY
BOOKS
A TRIBUNE NEW MEDIA COMPANY

Library of Congress Cataloging-in-Publication Data

Liebman, Glenn.
    Basketball shorts : 1,001 of the game's funniest
one-liners / Glenn Liebman.
        p.   cm.
    Includes index.
    ISBN 0-8092-3350-9 (alk. paper)
    1. Basketball—United States—Quotations,
maxims, etc.   2. Basketball players—United
States—Quotations.   I. Title.
GV885.7.L54   1995
796.323'0973—dc20   95-21574
                                                CIP

Published by Contemporary Books, Inc.
Two Prudential Plaza, Chicago, Illinois 60601-6790
Manufactured in the United States of America
International Standard Book Number: 0-8092-3350-9
10   9   8   7   6   5   4   3   2   1

To Kathy, for always being there as my
inspiration and my best friend

And to Frankie, for bringing us such
joy and happiness

ACKNOWLEDGMENTS

First of all, I must thank the Basketball Humor
Hall of Famers who made this book possible: Frank
Layden, Charles Barkley, Al McGuire, Abe Lemons,
Pat Williams, George Raveling, Jerry Reynolds, and
hundreds of others.

I would like to thank my agent, Philip Spitzer,
for his continued great work on behalf of the
Shorts series, and my editor at Contemporary
Books, Nancy Crossman, the guiding and integral
force behind this entire series of books.

Also, thanks to the usual assortment of
wonderful people in my life: my in-laws, Bill and
Helen Coll, and Granny Murray, who have helped to
make the Shorts series the top-selling books in
upstate New York; my friend Lou, a former
basketball fanatic ("Robisch shooting from the
outside, let me see that"); the Herbachs, who made
Kathy, Frankie, and me feel like members of their

family; and my friend Joe Gentile, who has taught me a great deal about management skills and life.

While on the subject of life lessons, I'd like to thank my dad, Bernard, who impressed on me the most important lesson in life—persevere and never give in to life's many obstacles—and my late mother, Frieda, who taught me to enjoy life and to treasure family and friends. I'd also like to thank my brother, Bennett, the man responsible for my love of sports, and his wonderful family—Deb, Samantha, and little Joy-Joy.

As always, the true inspiration for any book I've written is Kathy. After nine years, I am still amazed that someone so attractive, smart, and caring is married to me. You can also add wonderful mother to that list of qualities.

Finally, I'd like to thank the newest member of our family and a future member of the New York Knicks, circa 2016 (unless he decides to attend Yale Medical School), Frankie Jay. In my unbiased opinion, he is easily the greatest little kid in the history of the world. He has added a great deal of fun, laughter, joy, and inspiration to our lives. Plus, at six months old the little guy has developed a hell of a jump shot.

INTRODUCTION

For most of my teenage years, basketball was my life. From age 14 through 18, I spent most of my time on the same street corner with the same cast of characters: my buddies Dougie Brandwin (Mr. Rebounder) and Saul Kreps (Mr. Smooth); David Frank (Mr. Classic Jump Shot), Mitch Rappaport (Mr. Inside), and Robert Garfinkle (Mr. Fade-Away Jumper—even on a 3-on-1 break, he'd still stop and take that fade-away jump shot); and occasionally Steve Gentile, one of the studs on a pretty good high school basketball team. (The best player on that high school team was a tenth-grader named Frank Viola, who wisely gave up the game for another sport that would make him a millionaire.) I was known as Mr. Defense, a euphemism for having a lousy shot.

We were latchkey kids before anyone knew what the phrase meant. Every day from late August to November, and then again from March to June, we'd be outside playing game after game. The only real skill needed was a prehistoric, Long Island version of trash talk: "Nice shot, fat boy," "You shoot just like Hawthorne Wingo," or the ever-popular "Pass the ball, pimple puss." After playing on the corner all day, Dougie, Saul, my best buddy David Agler, and I often would spend the evening in my backyard shooting hoops and talking about dreams, ambitions, girls, popularity, sports, politics, television—almost anything except, God forbid, schoolwork.

I hope that my son, Frankie, will someday have his own wonderful memories of the camaraderie and the special friendships that are formed on the basketball court.

Needless to say, I relished the opportunity to work on a basketball book. The names of many of the coaches, players, and scribes quoted in these pages have been familiar to me for most of my life. Also, they are among the funniest characters in sports. For example:

Frank Layden, on his high school playing days in Brooklyn: "We had a lot of nicknames—Scarface, Blackie, Toothless. And those were just the cheerleaders."

Pat Williams, the G.M. of the Orlando Magic, on the huge contract signed by NBA Commissioner David Stern: "All I know is that on airline trips, David's wallet will be considered carry-on baggage."

Charles Barkley, on why the name of his sneakers was changed from Air Charles to Air Max: "So people who hate me will still buy them."

The late Jim Valvano, on his alleged resemblance to Joe Namath: "The difference in Namath and me is that when you make the money he makes, they say you're ruggedly handsome. When you make the money I make, they say you have a big nose."

So sit back, relax, and enjoy the hoop world's funniest one-liners. It sure beats *The Miracle of Helium*, which was Pat Williams's favorite book of the year. Why? Simply because he "couldn't put it down."

BASKETBALL
SHORTS

"There were the inevitable comparisons from day one. But they ended on day two."

> *Len Elmore, on replacing Lew*
> *Alcindor at center for Power*
> *Memorial (New York) High School*

"Give him the ball."

> *Magic Johnson, asked what he*
> *learned playing alongside Kareem*
> *during his rookie year*

"I'd get real close to him and breathe on his goggles."

> *Johnny Kerr, on the best way to stop*
> *Abdul-Jabbar*

"It'll be like Halloween without Elvira."

> *Mychal Thompson, on Abdul-Jabbar's*
> *retirement plans*

"You don't elbow the King. If you elbow the King, they throw you in the dungeon."

> *Mychal Thompson, asked why he didn't retaliate after Abdul-Jabbar elbowed him in practice*

ACADEMIC LIFE

"The only way I can make five A's is when I sign my name."

> *Alaa Abdelnaby, on his academic career at Duke*

"As long as I was leading the SEC in rebounding, my grades would be fine."

> *Charles Barkley, on his grades at Auburn*

"No, but they gave me one anyway."

> *Elden Campbell, asked if he earned his degree at Clemson*

"I'd say I gave it the old college try, except that I never went to college."

> *Darryl Dawkins, after a good game*

"How many other team buses have discussions on the implications of a negative income tax?"

> *Adam Keefe, on his college years at Stanford*

"Several."

> *Darryl Kennedy, Oklahoma player, asked what was his least-favorite class*

"When I picked the course for them, I didn't realize that the instructor graded on a curve and that there were 24 Indians in the class."

> *Abe Lemons, asked how two of his players failed basketweaving*

"Our guys took Shop and Advanced Shop. Shop is when you make a chair. Advanced Shop is when you paint it."

> *Al McGuire, on his days at Marquette*

"Son, it looks to me like you are spending too much time on one subject."

> *Shelby Metcalf, former Texas A&M basketball coach, on a student who made four F's and a D*

"Only Thomas Edison could invent a course Washburn could pass."

> *Jim Murray, on Chris Washburn getting an SAT score of 470 but still getting into North Carolina State*

"I understand the show *That's Incredible* has been filming on the USC campus. They shot 12 football players attending classes at the same time."

> *George Raveling*

"That leaves out three people on the East Coast."

> *Jim Valvano, offering a scholarship to his alma mater, Rutgers, for anyone who had a higher college GPA*

ADVERTISEMENTS

"Making commercials is repetitious. You have to do the same thing over and over. Ain't no commercial that's fun to do. Ain't nothing fun to do over and over except sex."

> *Charles Barkley*

"So people who hate me will still buy them."
> *Charles Barkley, asked why the name*
> *of his new sneakers was changed*
> *from Air Charles to Air Max*

"I could do a Primatene Mist commercial."
> *Shaquille O'Neal, on his breathing*
> *problems caused by asthma*

"The company should change its name to Mike."
> *Alvin Robertson, on all the ads*
> *Michael Jordan does for Nike*

AGE BEFORE BEAUTY

"I wish I was young again. I'd make a fortune and the coach couldn't yell at me."
> *Charles Barkley*

"They're so old we use Geritol instead of Gatorade."
> *Tom Chapman, coach at Gannon*
> *State, where his team included two*
> *Army veterans and a 30-year-old*

"We had a hot Geritol and went from there."
> *Bill Fitch, 60-year-old Clippers*
> *coach, after playing against 63-year-*
> *old Mavericks coach Dick Motta*

"I'm too old for games like this."
> *Al Fleming, freshman year at*
> *Arizona, after a triple-overtime game*

"I told my wife three years ago that my goal was to be a head coach by the age of 30. My goal now is to still be a head coach at the age of 30."
> *Greg Kampe, 28-year-old basketball*
> *coach at Oakland University in*
> *Michigan*

"The only thing old on me is this bald spot, and I'll have that fixed the next time we're in L.A."
> *John Lucas, on still playing at the*
> *age of 36*

"When Dr. Naismith put up the peach basket, Ray Meyer was holding his ladder."
> *Al McGuire, on the 42-year coaching*
> *career of DePaul's Meyer*

"There are three stages in life—youth, adulthood, and you look good. I'm in the last stage."
Ray Meyer

"Hey, I don't want to be Mister yet. My body is aging fast, but I'm staying immature enough to keep my mentality at a low level."
Doug Moe, on why he hates being called Mister

"We're so young, we have to stop practice every four minutes to change diapers."
Bob Reinhardt, on his young team at Georgia State

"Fifty-year-old women don't look like they're 50 to me anymore. They used to look like my grandmother—now they look like somebody you'd like to be seen with."
Donnie Walsh, Pacers president, on getting older

AGENTS

"If God had an agent, the world wouldn't be built yet. It'd only be about Thursday."

Jerry Reynolds

"What do you have when you've got an agent buried up to his neck in sand? . . . Not enough sand."

Pat Williams

AIRPLANES

"I didn't even know anything happened. I was dreaming of showgirls."

Anderson Hunt, UNLV player, after learning his plane to North Carolina almost made an emergency landing

"I just read the other day about a train that overturned—132 injured, 12 killed . . . A plane fell on it."

> *Johnny Kerr, trying to ease teammate*
> *Connie Dierking's fear of flying*

"I don't think we would have won that game if we didn't have that plane."

> *Dick Motta, on the importance of the*
> *Kings having a private jet with a*
> *road record of 1–40*

"I've never heard of a plane that backed into a mountain."

> *C. M. Newton, on why he takes the*
> *last seat in a plane*

"When I left Pullman International [airport in Washington], I asked the baggage handler to send one bag to Seattle, one to Portland, and the other to Billings, Montana. He said, 'I can't do that.' I said, 'Why not? You did it two years ago.'"

> *George Raveling*

"When you're from Pullman, you're happy to be going anywhere."

> *George Raveling, on a trip to Alaska during his coaching days at Washington State University*

"They had a $100-a-plate dinner for Ronald Reagan while we were there. We figured we'd make it our pregame meal. It's just as cheap as ordering off the menu."

> *Jim Valvano, on a tournament in Alaska*

ALL-AMERICANS

"He was a high-school All-American, but there weren't a hell of a lot of Americans in those days."

> *George Raveling, on Ralph Miller, former Oregon State basketball coach who retired at age 69*

"He wants to vote and cheat on his taxes like everyone else."

> *Mychal Thompson, on how Vlade*
> *Divac wants to be a good American*

"No, but we do have an all-conference guard."

> *Members of the Whitman College*
> *basketball team, asked at the*
> *Canadian border if they were all*
> *American*

ALL-STAR GAME

"Where the hell can you find good links in Minnesota in February? I've gotta have a chat with David [Stern]. He's gotta start putting these things in Phoenix, L.A., or Florida. So I can golf 36 holes."

> *Charles Barkley, complaining about*
> *the 1994–95 All-Star Game site*

"I don't know. But my hands are tired from stuffing the ballots."

> *Cedric Ceballos, on his chances of*
> *making the 1994–95 All-Star Team*

11

"If you don't make the All-Star Team, what am I paying you all that money for?"

> *Stan Kasten, Hawks GM, to Dominique Wilkins, who was negotiating for a contract that paid him more for making the All-Star Team*

"I'll always be number one to myself. The legend just won't be there. I guess I'll go home and watch my own videos."

> *Moses Malone, on not being voted to the All-Star Team after 12 straight appearances*

"The two games I played in the ABA, the losers got 50 dollars apiece."

> *Swen Nater, on the difference between making the NBA All-Star Team and making the ABA All-Star Team*

"A good coach is a coach who can be chased down the street by irate alumni and make it look as if he's leading a parade."

Tom Brock, former coach at
University of Omaha

"I was so bad that when I shook hands with boosters, they took money out of my hand."

Scott Hastings, on his days at the
University of Arkansas

"They wanted to buy up my contract, but neither had change for 20 dollars."

Abe Lemons, on two alumni who
were dissatisfied with his
performance

"I left my last job because of a health problem. The alumni were sick of me."

Sonny Smith, coach of Virginia
Commonwealth University

APPLAUSE, APPLAUSE

"Give them time. They'll learn."
> *Rich Kelley, on being given a*
> *standing ovation after being traded*
> *to Phoenix*

ASSISTS

"If one of our guys misses a layup and the next guy
taps it in, I say to the first guy, 'Nice assist.'"
> *Norm Stewart, on developing a better*
> *perspective on life after battling*
> *cancer*

"When I've been making the pass, the guys haven't
been making the shot. I've been looking."
> *Eddie Lee Wilkins, on getting no*
> *assists in his first 27 games*

"I know the guys are out there somewhere; I just
don't know where."
> *Buck Williams, on averaging fewer*
> *than 2 assists per game for his career*

ATTENDANCE

"It's a partial sellout."

> *Skip Caray, on a crowd of 3,600 at*
> *Richfield Coliseum for a*
> *Hawks–Cavaliers game*

"At least now I can find my wife in the crowd."

> *Joe C. Meriweather, on the*
> *advantages of small crowds at*
> *Kansas City Kings games*

AWARDS

"After I got the call from New York, five minutes later my wife had me take the garbage out."

> *Frank Layden, on the respect he*
> *received for being named Coach of*
> *the Year*

"The game needs somebody like Michael to liven it up. All these players are so mediocre. Hit .230 and you make $3 million."

> *Charles Barkley, after Michael Jordan announced that he would pursue a baseball career*

"I can't scratch my nose when he's in the game. He still thinks it means bunt."

> *Bill Fitch, on former major leaguer Danny Ainge*

"There's something odd about going up to Michael Jordan and slipping him 16 dollars a day."

> *Terry Francona, Jordan's minor league manager, on giving him his daily meal money*

"They asked me to say something nice about Tommy. All right, he doesn't shed."

> *Frank Layden, at a roast for Tommy Lasorda*

"The Babe Ruth of basketball has become the Lucy Layup of baseball."

> *Bernie Lincicome, Chicago Tribune columnist, on Michael Jordan being considered a singles hitter*

"After the season with the Celtics, he said he wouldn't pitch for the Red Sox for four weeks because it took him that long to get out of shape."

> *Bill Russell, on two-sport athlete Gene Conley*

"I got bored standing around chewing sunflower seeds."

> *Jimmy Soto, University of Utah basketball player who gave up baseball even though that was his better sport*

"Basically, the league is like everybody else that knows me. They haven't asked my opinion on anything. I've been shut out more than the old '52 Senators."

> *Charles Spoonhour, St. Louis University basketball coach, on a proposed All-Star sports league that would include St. Louis*

"In the NBA, nothing recedes like success."
Bob Cousy

"It's not how good you are when you play good. It's how good you are when you play bad. And we played pretty good, even though we played bad. Imagine if we played good."

> *Litterial Green, Georgia guard, after his team beat Georgia Tech by one point*

"Never trust a guy whose hair is perfect, who never sweats, says yessir and nossir all the time, and never says sumbitch."

> *Abe Lemons*

"Teaching basketball is like teaching a chicken how to bark. I once had a left-handed center, so left-handed he couldn't ring a doorbell with his right hand."

> *Abe Lemons, asked if it is possible to teach a kid basketball*

"To win, you've got to put the ball in the macramé."

> *Terry McGuire, wife of Dick*
> *McGuire, explaining the strategy of*
> *basketball*

"I played the game with an innate smile."

> *Earl Monroe, describing his*
> *enthusiasm for the game*

"The worst thing that could happen to a coach is having to play with all freshmen or sophomores. Second worst is having to play with all seniors."

> *C. M. Newton*

"I look at the NBA as a football game without the helmet."

> *Tom Tolbert*

"This is the second most exciting indoor sport, and the other one shouldn't have spectators."

> *Dick Vertleib, former Warriors GM*

WALT BELLAMY

"He's the skeleton in the closet of the 20,000-point club."

George Kiseda, sportswriter, on Walt Bellamy

BENCHWARMERS

"I should be out there."

Charles Barkley, asked what he learned from being the 76ers' sixth man in his rookie year

"If you're not going to play, you might as well not play for the best."

Jack Mansell, benchwarmer on fourth-ranked Georgia Tech

"Our bench is kind of like a video store late on Saturday night. There aren't a lot of choices."

Kevin O'Neill, Tennessee coach, on being forced to use his bench because of injuries suffered by several starters

"It wouldn't have happened if I started."
> *Rony Seikaly, on hurting his back
> while getting off the bench to enter
> a game*

"The secret is to have eight great players and four others who will cheer like crazy."
> *Jerry Tarkanian*

"Every team needs huggers. These are the guys you sign so you can hug 'em after you won instead of having to hug the guys who play and sweat."
> *Tommy Varden, assistant basketball
> coach at Centenary, on backup
> players*

BENOIT BENJAMIN

"George is very egotistical. He went so far as to say that I was an LP in his CD collection."
> *Benoit Benjamin, on George Karl, his
> former coach*

"The earth in L.A. moved more in one hour than Benoit Benjamin did all last season with the Clippers."

> *Peter Vecsey, on an earthquake in Los Angeles*

BIRD MAN

"When you got a Mercedes—you drive it."

> *Charles Barkley, on Larry Bird being criticized by teammates for continuing to shoot during a slump*

"He could never shoot a two-handed set shot."

> *John Havlicek, asked if there was anything Bird couldn't do on the court*

"I never noticed that Bird was black or white. I didn't even know he was human."

> *Frank Layden, on Isiah Thomas's comment that if Bird were black, he would be regarded as an average player*

"I told Robert we'll probably get ours during a 20-second time-out."

> *Kevin McHale, comparing the*
> *ceremony he and Robert Parish will*
> *get when they retire with that of Bird*

"The greatest white player to play a black man's sport."

> *Mychal Thompson*

"Big Bird is more like it."

> *Wes Unseld, on people comparing*
> *Tom Gugliotta to Larry Bird*

"Any living legend can take a game over in the last few minutes. Only Bird can take it over in the first few minutes."

> *Peter Vecsey*

BLOCKED SHOTS

"When Divac rejects a shot, it should be known as the Eastern Bloc."

> *Tom Plate, editorial director of the*
> L.A. Times, *on Vlade Divac, formerly*
> *of Yugoslavia*

MANUTE BOL

"He's so thin, the 76ers don't bother to take him on the road—they just fax him from town to town."

> *Woody Allen*

"He's so tall that if he falls down, he'd be halfway home."

> *Darryl Dawkins*

"I don't know why NASA spends all that money on the space shuttle. All they've got to do is send Manute some tools and let him reach up and fix things."

> *Mychal Thompson*

"Now, I'm certain he killed that lion with a free throw."

Peter Vecsey, on the legend that Bol killed a lion

"He's so skinny, his pajamas have only one pinstripe."

Pat Williams

"He looks like he went to the blood bank and forgot to say when."

Pat Williams

BOOK BEAT

"That was my fault. I should have read it before it came out."

Charles Barkley, on being misquoted in his autobiography

"If all his old girlfriends buy it, it'll be a best-seller."

Hot Rod Hundley's ex-wife, on his autobiography

"I couldn't put it down."

> *Pat Williams, on why* The Miracle of Helium *was his favorite book*

"Charles once told me he would write his autobiography as soon as he could figure out who the major character would be."

> *Pat Williams, on Charles Barkley*

SAM BOWIE

"He's our Manute [Bol]. Without him, we're minute."

> *Mychal Thompson, on the injury suffered by Trailblazers' teammate Sam Bowie*

"Save those bricks for your business."

> *Charlie Criss, to Harvey Catchings, owner of a construction company who threw up a lot of bricks during a game*

"We have a great bunch of outside shooters. Unfortunately, all our games are played indoors."

> *Weldon Drew, New Mexico State coach*

"They throw up enough bricks during warm-ups to build a condominium."

> *Bill Foster, on his players when he was coaching at the University of Miami*

"I could hear groans from the crowd when we were getting ready to shoot."

> *Andy Russo, University of Washington coach, on a bad shooting game by his team*

"It's so bad that the players are giving each other high fives when they hit the rim."

> Ron Shumate, Southeastern Missouri coach, on his team's poor shooting

BROADWAY

"There are only two great plays—put the ball in the basket and *South Pacific*."

> Charley Eckman, coach of the now-defunct Fort Wayne Pistons, on his coaching philosophy

"Baryshnikov was great, but the play needs a shot clock."

> Bucky Waters, on a production of the play Metamorphosis *starring Mikhail Baryshnikov*

DALE BROWN

"I looked down the floor and saw Dale Brown and I knew we had a chance."

> *Bobby Knight, on beating LSU after being down by 12 points with 12 minutes left*

LARRY BROWN

"I wanted to be like Larry Brown. I walked like him. I talked like him. I even moved three times."
> *Billy Crystal*

"Larry Brown is like Liz Taylor. Just when you think it's over, someone new is ready to walk her down the aisle."
> *Donnie Walsh*

"I thought it was a bad dream. Did he want to see how much damage he did to the team? He needs to apologize."

> *Terry Davis, on Buckner showing up*
> *for a Mavericks exhibition game after*
> *being fired as the coach*

BY THE TIME CHARLES GETS TO PHOENIX

"Phoenix is not a bad place. I can play golf every day."

> *Charles Barkley, asked his reaction*
> *to being traded to the Suns*

"Before, there were a lot of old people waiting to die."

> *Charles Barkley, on the influence*
> *that he and Arizona Cardinals head*
> *coach Buddy Ryan have had on*
> *Phoenix*

CAN YOU TELL ME HOW TO GET TO SESAME STREET?

"When kids say they are visiting North Carolina, Duke, Kentucky, Kansas, and Florida State University, it's almost like that Sesame Street song, 'Which of these things doesn't belong here?'"

Pat Kennedy, Florida State coach, on the respect FSU receives as a college basketball power

C B A

"Sometimes I think the CBA is there only to give you the inspiration to get out of there."

Milt Newton, former NBA player

"But I've been wrong before. I thought Mickey Rooney would be a bachelor."

> *Al McGuire, on disagreeing with a foul call*

"I have always admired his training methods and devotion, but I didn't have the guts to tell him his acting stinks."

> *Bill Musselman, on meeting Chuck Norris*

"The difference in Namath and me is that when you make the money he makes, they say you're ruggedly handsome. When you make the money I make, they say you have a big nose."

> *Jim Valvano, on being told he looks like Joe Namath*

"I've had more engagements than Mickey Rooney."

> *Bob Wenzel, on giving his thirty-fifth speech after being named coach of Jacksonville*

"They don't buy all those banners at Woolworth."
Kareem Abdul-Jabbar, on all the championship banners at Boston Garden

CENTER OF ATTENTION

"It's good because now people can't get on me when I shoot outside. They can't say, 'A center shouldn't take those shots.' "
Vlade Divac, on being converted to a power forward

"The 76ers need a center in the worst way. And Dana Lewis is a center in the worst way."
Jack Kiser, sportswriter, on the 1971 76ers draft choice

"If the NBA takes Patrick Ewing, Alonzo Mourning, and Mutombo to South Africa for the next five years, no kids will know how to dribble or shoot."
Dikembe Mutombo

"If we had one more center, we'd have one."

Jerry Reynolds, on the Sacramento Kings

CHARLES IN CHARGE

"I have very few friends I have met since I became Charles Barkley."

Charles Barkley, on why he hangs out with old friends

"I was going to sue her for defamation of character, but then I realized I have no character."

Charles Barkley, on Tonya Harding calling herself the Charles Barkley of ice-skating

"When you're the top dog, everybody wants to put you in the pound."

Charles Barkley, on his greatness

"Lots of people look up to Charles Barkley. That's because he's just knocked them down."

Chuck Daly

"I don't wince anymore at anything he says. I am winced out."

> *Matt Guokas, former 76ers coach, on Charles*

"Maybe I need to write a book and say I was misquoted, or punch somebody in Milwaukee."

> *Michael Jordan, on Barkley's being ahead of Jordan in the All-Star balloting*

"He's never won no more than I won. He's got the same number of rings I got—zero."

> *Xavier McDaniel, responding to Barkley, who called him untalented*

"Not that much, I hope."

> *Paul Westphal, asked how much influence Charles had on fellow Auburn alumnus Wesley Person*

CHRISTMASTIME
IN THE CITY

"If ifs were gifts, every day would be Christmas."
Charles Barkley

CLIPPERS

"I call L.A. the city of alternatives. If you don't like mountains, we got the ocean. If you don't like Knott's Berry Farm, we've got Disney World. If you don't like basketball, we've got the Clippers."
Arsenio Hall

"Nobody's as stupid as me. Nobody's going to invest in this team."

> *Donald Sterling, Clippers owner, on possible investors*

"They're already talking about changing coaches. They're considering this guy from China. His name is Win Won Soon."

> *Pat Williams, on the early-1994 losing streak of the Clippers*

"With all these guys in suits and ties on the bench, the sideline was beginning to look like the men's shop at Macy's."

Dale Brown, on coaching-staff cuts

"It's great to see Pinky Lee's estate has finally been settled."

Bob Costas, on Wimp Sanderson's multicolored sports jackets

"Look, show me something for about 300 dollars for a sheep that fooled around a little."

Chuck Daly, after rejecting a $1,300 virgin wool suit

"We had to go to Toys 'R' Us."

Bob Ferry, on clothes-shopping for 5'3" Muggsy Bogues

"If I ever lose my luggage, I know where to go to borrow clothes."

Mike Fratello, 5'7" former Hawks coach, on the advantages of coaching 5'7" Spud Webb

"The dry-cleaning bill."

> *Kathi Hahn, asked what came to mind when she saw her husband Billy's wild antics as Ohio University coach*

"I'm fat and I sweat a lot and don't want to ruin all my clothes."

> *Don Haskins, on why he wears the same clothes all the time*

"They pass from the homely to the homeless."

> *Judd Heathcote, on donating his famous green jackets to Goodwill after he wears them*

"I learned to hate plaid."

> *Mike Krzyzewski, asked what he learned as Bobby Knight's assistant*

"He spends more on a haircut than I do on a sports jacket."

> *Frank Layden, comparing his sartorial style with that of Pat Riley*

"We're both Irish and we're both from New York and we're both good looking. The only difference is that he has his clothes tailored and I find mine."

Frank Layden, again comparing himself with Riley

"You could house 20 homeless families in them."

Rick Majerus, heavyweight coach, on his sweaters

"Even if you took him to Paris, you couldn't find clothes for him."

Dick Motta, on Frank Layden

"Looie could do for sweater sales what the Boston Strangler did for door-to-door salesmen."

Bucky Waters, on Lou Carnesecca's choice of unusual sweaters

COACHING

"I have two college degrees, but the only way I could ever make a living was by showing kids how to put a ball in a hole."

Red Auerbach

"Coaching is easy. Winning is the hard part."
Elgin Baylor

"If you don't look like Robert Redford and if you aren't funny like Johnny Carson and if you don't have thick skin like an elephant and if you don't win as much as the Harlem Globetrotters, you aren't going to last very long."
Jim Crews, coach at Evansville, on longevity in coaching

"Maybe I could have continued if I worked at a prison or an orphanage. A prison doesn't have organized alumni, and an orphanage doesn't have meddling parents."
Johnny Dee, former Notre Dame coach, on why he gave up coaching

"I don't know much about psychology. Then again, I don't know much about coaching."
Don Donoher, Dayton coach, asked if he tried to psych out officials

"All it means is that when they fire me as coach, it won't be by a unanimous vote."

> *Mike Fratello, after being named vice president as well as coach of the Hawks*

"Old coaches don't fade away, they just smell that way."

> *Dr. Tom Haggai, former Furman coach*

"Coaching is all I've ever done. I've never had a real job."

> *Jack Hartman, coach of Kansas State*

"The one thing about this game is that it makes fools of us all."

> *Judd Heathcote*

"Players today expect coaches to be the chauffeurs. Coaches have to drive the way the players tell them to drive, or else. It's ridiculous."

> *Tommy Heinsohn*

"The coach who thinks his coaching is more important than his talent is an idiot."

Joe Lapchick

"If you gave Michelangelo bad marble, he couldn't make a great statue. You've got to have good material."

Frank Layden, on the importance of having good players

"The first thing I learned upon becoming a head coach after fifteen years as an assistant was the enormous difference between making a suggestion and making a decision."

Rick Majerus

"Going for 1,000 wins is not so impressive. It's losing 750 games and still getting a job. If you ask me, that's impressive."

Dick Motta

"It gives you a nice warm feeling to know you're the highest-paid guy in the huddle."

Rick Pitino, on the difference between coaching in the pros and at the college level

"He's what we call a contact coach, all con and no tact."

Bob Reinhart, on Billy Tubbs

"I've been convinced for some time that the Lord is punishing me for past transgressions, and I was a pretty ornery little guy. But it seems to me that I may be getting blamed for other Jerry Reynoldses too."

Jerry Reynolds, on his ups and downs as coach of the Kings

"I've been here so long that when I got here the Dead Sea wasn't even sick."

Wimp Sanderson, on his long tenure at Alabama

"I learned a long time ago to have one with three kids. He'll be in his office working at eight every morning so he doesn't have to deal with getting the kids off to school."

Dick Versace, on how he hires assistant coaches

"I've paid my dues. I've coached in places elephants go to die."

Dick Versace

43

"Some would say it was a measure of endurance; some would say it was a measure of insanity. Depending on the day, I would agree with both."

> *Paul Webb, Old Dominion coach, on winning 500 games*

"I spent five seasons of my life coaching two seasons of NBA ball."

> *Tex Winter, on his tenure as Houston Rockets coach*

COMEBACK

"The only person who's had a bigger comeback than Bagley is Lazarus."

> *Kevin McHale, on the resurgent play of John Bagley*

"The head of the Colombian cartel doesn't make that much money."

> *Frank Layden, on David Stern's*
> *$27.5 million contract*

"All I know is that on airline trips, David's wallet will be considered carry-on baggage."

> *Pat Williams, after the terms of*
> *Stern's contract were revealed*

"David's son asked him to buy a chemistry set, so David went out and bought Du Pont."

> *Pat Williams*

"David is now buying a house in a neighborhood where kids play Little League polo and the Salvation Army has a string section."

> *Pat Williams*

COMMUNICATIONS BREAKDOWN

"I kept feeling like the Hindu snake charmer with a deaf cobra."

> *Bill Fitch, on not being able to*
> *communicate with his players during*
> *a tough loss*

"Anytime you see him wink at you, you can be sure he hasn't got a clue."

> *Mark McNamara, on trying to*
> *communicate with Vlade Divac*

COMPLAIN, COMPLAIN

"I'm not a complainer. I'm a whiner."

> *Danny Ainge, defending himself*
> *against those who say he complains*
> *all the time*

"I've checked into Waters Anonymous in Salt Lake City for rehabilitation."

> *Danny Ainge, on his reputation as a crybaby*

"When they do that, I just ask myself, 'What did I expect, Boys Town?'"

> *Stu Jackson, former Knicks coach, on players complaining about playing time*

"There is no such thing as coulda, shoulda, woulda. If you shoulda and coulda, you woulda."

> *Pat Riley*

CONSISTENCY

"Our consistency has been up and down all season."

> *Robert Parish, discussing an inconsistent Celtics season*

"We wanted to put together 40 minutes of basketball. We did. We put together 40 solid minutes of bad basketball."

Bobby Paschal, Southwestern Louisiana coach, after losing a game by 25 points

"Hey, take it easy. We're not brewing instant coffee around here."

Dick Versace, on a great early-season winning streak for the Pacers

CRIME AND PUNISHMENT

"I got the superstar treatment. Everybody else got bologna and water. I got bologna and milk."

Charles Barkley, on the four hours he spent in a Milwaukee prison

"There was no place I could go to cut classes."

Marvin Barnes, on why he earned a lot of college credits in prison

"I should have told them about the color TV and Steinway piano I always carry."

> *David Magley, Cavaliers forward, on receiving a $1,000 insurance check after his hotel room was burglarized*

DEATH BE NOT PROUD

"I gave in another life."

> *Rich Kelley, after a group of Hare Krishnas asked him for a donation at the airport*

"That was the nail that broke the coffin's back."

> *Jack Kraft, former Villanova coach, on one of his top players fouling out*

"You did great, son. You scored one more point than a dead man."

> *Abe Lemons, to his star player, who had scored one point in a game*

"Hell no. If I die, I want to be sick."

> *Abe Lemons, asked if he wanted to take up jogging*

"Their pulse is fading fast. Better call a priest."

Cedric Maxwell, on the Celtics leading the 76ers 3–1 in an NBA semifinal series

"I was able to send my girlfriend flowers every day."

Digger Phelps, on the advantages of having a father who's a mortician

"The biggest scare for me was the thought of Billy Jones [the trainer] giving me mouth-to-mouth resuscitation. Death is preferable."

Jerry Reynolds, on fainting on the sidelines during a game

"If you make every game a life-and-death thing, you're going to have problems. You'll be dead a lot."

Dean Smith

"Basketball doesn't owe me anything. It has been very good to me. It's just that most folks who remember me are dead."

Tex Winter, 72-year-old assistant coach, on why he is never considered for the Hall of Fame

"We deny everything."

> *Tom Asbury, Pepperdine coach, on*
> *naming his defense "The Clarence"*
> *after Supreme Court Justice Clarence*
> *Thomas*

"We have forty-four defenses for him, but he has forty-five ways to score."

> *Al Attles, on how his team tries to*
> *defend Nate "Tiny" Archibald*

"That usually means you can't shoot."

> *Hosie Grimsley, Florida guard, after*
> *being named one of the top five*
> *defenders in college basketball by*
> *Dick Vitale*

"Tony Campbell might be the NBA's defensive player of the year, if everybody else dies."

> *Chick Hearn*

"I took advantage of the absence of his presence."

Michael Jordan, after having a big game in the absence of top defensive player Dennis Johnson

"That's the first person he defended this year."

Craig Kilborn, ESPN commentator, on Don MacLean defending his girlfriend during a fight

"I'm a defensive coach. I couldn't shoot when I played, so I teach defense."

Al McGuire

"People keep saying we are the worst defensive team in the league. Actually we are second—our opponents are the worst."

Doug Moe, on the Nuggets averaging 126.5 points a game while opponents averaged 126

"I hate it. It looks like a stickup at 7-Eleven. Five guys standing there with their hands in the air."

Norm Sloan, on the zone defense

"Tree could be the only player in college basketball who can keep both teams in the game at the same time."

> *Jack Spencer, Nevada–Reno assistant coach, on Ken "Tree" Spencer, a prolific scorer but a terrible defensive player*

"I don't know if we play D or not, but I'd like to hear what those 30 teams we beat were playing."

> *Billy Tubbs, commenting on the defense of offensive-minded Oklahoma*

DENTAL PLAN

"If you hang in there long enough and grit your teeth hard enough, your orthodontist bill will go up."

> *Stan Morrison, former USC coach*

"My wife is a dentist, so I wouldn't say that."

> *Andy Russo, University of Washington coach, asked if facing #1 Arizona was like visiting the dentist*

"We win, or the alumni bash in our teeth."
Jim Valvano, explaining the dental
plan at North Carolina State

DICKIE V

"He's the car alarm siren that can't be stopped. He's the Lhasa apso barking at your feet. He's the skip in the record that plays over and over."
Norman Chad, on Dick Vitale

"I knew that if he shot off his mouth long enough, he'd say something right."
Billy Tubbs, on Vitale calling Tubbs
an offensive genius

DIRTY PLAY

"He's not even good enough to be dirty."
Danny Ainge, on Greg Anthony

"Covering Bird, my legs were worn out. Covering Kareem, my elbows are worn out."

Caldwell Jones

"Sam Lacey says I'm a dirty player, but I tell him I take a lot of showers."

Swen Nater

"The Pistons were very hospitable to Rony. They welcomed him with open arms and closed arms and forearms."

Ron Rothstein, former Heat coach, on the Pistons' play against Rony Seikaly

DISCIPLINE

"It was Sunday night and everything was shut down. I'd be doing them a favor by letting them come in early."

Abe Lemons, on letting his players stay out till 10 P.M. in Abilene

"When I discipline them, I make them play."
Abe Lemons, on a fellow coach who
disciplined a top player by forcing
him to sit out a game

"I have only one training rule—don't get caught."
Frank McGuire

DISSENSION

"Harmony isn't important. The only thing that matters is winning and getting paid."
Charles Barkley

"We all need to join hands and sing 'Kumbaya.'"
Brian Williams, on rumors of
dissension on the Nuggets

"Coaches are always under the gun. I'd like to see the won-lost records of doctors out front where people could see for themselves. Won 10, lost 3, tied 2."

Abe Lemons

"Doctors bury their mistakes. We still have ours on scholarship."

Abe Lemons

"Finish last in your league and they call you idiot. Finish last in medical school and they call you doctor."

Abe Lemons

"Remember, half the doctors in the country graduated in the bottom half of their class."

Al McGuire, on why athletes shouldn't be criticized for academic problems

"During practice or games, if I made a mistake Billy was on my ass before I knew anything was wrong. But if Doc committed the very same mistake, Billy wouldn't say a word. All of a sudden Billy C's Ray C—Ray Charles."

> *Charles Barkley, on Coach Billy Cunningham's preferential treatment of Julius Erving*

"I'm the bad guy. You got your good guys, your Dr. J. You got your pie-and-ice-cream guys. I'm no pie-and-ice-cream guy."

> *Marvin Barnes*

"The only problem I had with the wall is that I had to climb it. Doc just jumped onto it."

> *M. L. Carr, on touring the Great Wall of China with Dr. J*

"The thing about him is that you know he is going to get to the basket—you just don't know how."

> *Bobby Jones, on Julius Erving*

"There have been some better people off the court—
like a few mothers and the pope. But there was
only one Dr. J the player."
Pat Riley

DRAFT DAY

"If you don't get lucky, you just sit there like a big
dork."

*Don Nelson, on the NBA draft lottery
program*

"What happens to me next year will happen to me
no matter what happens."
Bryant Reeves, on the NBA draft

"The good news is there are a lot of good second-
round picks. The bad news is a lot will go in the
first round."
Jerry Reynolds, on the 1990 draft

"I have no preference. That's his job."

> *Scotty Robertson, Pistons coach,*
> *asked whether General Manager Jack*
> *McCloskey should go for heads or*
> *tails to decide who gets the first pick*
> *in the draft*

DREAM TEAM

"What do I know about Cuba? The country is run by a scruffy-looking guy who smokes cigars. That's all I know."

> *Charles Barkley, on facing Cuba in*
> *the '92 Olympics*

"Laimbeer couldn't make the Czechoslovakian Olympic team."

> *Frank Layden, on Bill Laimbeer*
> *criticizing the USA Olympic*
> *Committee selection process*

"Imagine the road to New Orleans starting in a bathroom."

> *Gary Leonard, Missouri center, on having a drug test before the beginning of an NCAA Tournament in which the Final Four was played in New Orleans*

"I'm in favor of it as long as it's multiple choice."
> *Kurt Rambis*

"It was the only thing I could not fill out all night."
> *Garde Thompson, after scoring 33 points in a game and then having problems with his urine test*

DUKE

"I go up on a mountaintop, and I see a guy in a Duke hat. I then go play golf in Palm Springs, and I see another guy in a Duke hat. . . . If Grant Hill is tired of lack of respect, he should come to West Lafayette with me."

Gene Keady, Purdue coach,
responding to Grant Hill's charge
that Duke does not get any respect

"They're all from Jersey, so they sound like me."
Jim Valvano, on Duke fans

DUNKS

"The Chocolate Thunder Flying Robinzine Crying, Teeth Shaking, Glass Breaking, Rump Roasting, Bun Toasting, Wham, Bam, I Am Jam."

Darryl Dawkins, describing his dunk
after breaking a backboard

"When I dunk, I put something on it. I want the ball to hit the floor before I do."

Darryl Dawkins

"When they're all dunks, you should make the most of them."

Mark Eaton, on hitting 10 shots in a row

"If you stay near the ground, you don't get hurt."

Bill Hanzlik, on the advantage the Nuggets had in having the fewest dunks in the NBA

"I don't know whether I'll fly or not. I know that when I'm in the air, sometimes I feel like I don't ever have to come down."

Michael Jordan

"Yes, but you have to provide your own trampoline."

Brian McIntyre, NBA VP, on the aging Johnny Kerr's request to compete in the slam-dunk competition

"Maybe I need to work on my offense a little. But no one has played me one-on-one except Philadelphia, and I had 19 dunks."
> *Shaquille O'Neal*

"We could have brought the old alley-oop back to Boston Garden, except I can't really jump anymore, so I guess they would have to be alley-oop layups now."
> *Rony Seikaly, on playing in Boston with former Syracuse teammate Sherman Douglas*

"I ran out of dunks by halftime."
> *Dominique Wilkins, after Atlanta scored 194 points in an exhibition game*

ECONOMY

"They talk about the economy this year. Hey, my hairline is in recession, my waistline is in inflation. Altogether, I'm in a depression."
> *Rick Majerus*

"It's hard to tell what this card is worth. The supply is limited, but so is the demand."

> *Craig Sager, TNT host, on a special card made of him by HOOPS Basketball*

EGO

"They got me."

> *Charles Barkley, asked how the 76ers could play well without guard Johnny Dawkins*

"You're only as good as your limitations, and I don't have any."

> *Edgar Jones, former Cavaliers center*

"A team should be an extension of the coach's personality. My teams were arrogant and obnoxious."

> *Al McGuire*

"That's because I haven't had any yet. But when I do, I plan to get egotistical as all get-out."

> *Jerry Reynolds, asked why success*
> *hasn't gotten to his head*

"His head is so big he has to go through a car wash to get it clean."

> *John Salley, on Mark Aguirre*

"I like Frank Layden's autobiography—Famous Men Who Have Known Me."

> *Pat Williams*

ENGINEERS

"We don't win many games, but we could fix any gym we played in."

> *Gordon Chiesa, former Manhattan*
> *coach, on having four players on his*
> *team who were engineering students*

"Guys who should be shooting from 10 to 12 feet have been shooting from 15 to 16 feet. It's like somebody who wants to be an engineer but can't pass calculus."

> *Paul Hansen, former Oklahoma State coach*

ESPN

"If we had ESPN 22 years ago, we'd have never had any kids."

> *Terry Taux, basketball coach at Towson State, on watching basketball every night*

PATRICK EWING

"I saw my life pass in front of me."

> *Stu Jackson, former Knicks coach, after seeing Ewing fall to the floor and crack his ribs*

"We call it our Noriega Defense—every time Patrick turns around, he is surrounded by Americans."

Mychal Thompson, on the way the Lakers defense Ewing

EXERCISE

"I think if I went to Utah and got the head of the Mormon Tabernacle Choir, I'd have someone in better shape than Pete."

Bill Fitch, on an out-of-shape Pete Maravich

"I get a lot of practice just lifting myself out of bed every day."

Frank Layden, asked if he lifted weights

"I love exercise. I could watch it all day."

Bill Russell

EXPERIENCE

"I'd rather have older guys who are great players than younger guys who stink."

> *Charles Barkley, on why he respected the Celtics' older front line of Bird, McHale, and Parish*

"If you're dumb enough to coach for 25 years, you'll probably win 500 games. Winning 500 games just means you've been around for a while."

> *Lefty Driesell*

"I'd rather have a lot of talent and little experience than a lot of experience and little talent."

> *John Wooden*

FAMILY AFFAIR

"Philadelphia versus Milwaukee."

> *Ed Batojowski, former NBA referee, asked when his daughter was born*

"He looks a lot like his father, Dolph, but he plays more like his mother."

> *Skip Caray, on Danny Schayes, son of basketball Hall of Famer Dolph Schayes*

"Our family was big enough to be our own gang."

> *Terry Cummings, one of thirteen children, on why he never joined a gang when he was growing up*

"Michael's a special kind of kid. He's the kind of kid I'd want for my own son. I'd want him for my own son because he's going to make a lot of money."

> *Dave "Smokey" Gaines, on star player Michael Cage*

"I married her for her genes. I'm recruiting long term."

> *Lou Goetz, former Richmond coach, on marrying Tracy Groat, the daughter of former basketball All-American and baseball star Dick Groat*

"She deserves it for the product she put out."

Michael Jordan, on his mother's love of publicity

"I didn't hire Scott because he's my son. I hired him because I'm married to his mother."

Frank Layden, on hiring his son as an assistant coach

"I always say if I ever remarry, we'll live in a hotel with adjoining suites. If more couples do that, I guarantee the divorce rate will fall."

Rick Majerus

"The key for me is to have enough children so I have a better chance of one liking me and I'm able to move in with that one when I'm old."

Kevin McHale, on his wife expecting their fifth child

"She gave me some good advice. She told me to stay out of Cleveland."

Dan Roundfield, on asking his sister for advice after shooting 0-for-6 against the Cavaliers

"We were so poor, one time when a photographer took our family picture, he said 'Cheese' and we all lined up."

*Lafayette Stribbling, coach at
Mississippi Valley State*

"Just have them meet me on the first or the fifteenth of the month. Then there will be no doubt which Valvano is which."

*Bob Valvano, former Kutztown State
coach, on people who confused him
with his brother Jim*

"Are you any relation to your brother Marv?"

*Leon Wood, former NBA player,
introducing himself to announcer
Steve Albert*

"I want all you fans to remember when I shoot an airball, I want you to cheer me too."

> *Charles Barkley, on 16-year-old Michael Heban getting a standing ovation after shooting an air ball from three-point range that would have won him a million dollars*

"I like kids when they're kids. I don't like it when they grow up and come to the games and call you names."

> *Charles Barkley*

"I would have gone, but they didn't give me a destination."

> *Don DeVoe, former Florida coach, on hearing the chant "DeVoe must go"*

"Coaches who start listening to fans wind up sitting next to them."

> *Johnny Kerr*

"I thought they were doing a great job until they boosted me onto a platform that had a noose in the middle."

Frank Layden, on a booster club formed in Utah

"We formed a booster club in Utah, but by the end of the season it had turned into a terrorist group."

Frank Layden, on a bad season in Utah

"Maybe the fan was trying to tell me I stink."

Neal Morton, Michigan reserve, on a Right Guard deodorant stick landing at his feet during a game

"Our dinner table at home is more exciting, and two of our kids are gone."

Dick Motta, on the fans in Dallas

"I think fans say—'He's big, he can run, he's funny, he dives on the floor, he dunks with his left or right hand, and he's got lots of tricks in his bag.' If I was a fan, I'd come watch me play, too."

Shaquille O'Neal

"I appreciate the support, but I can't believe they ended a sentence with a preposition."

> *Walter Palmer, Utah Jazz player and*
> *Ivy League grad, on fans displaying*
> *a sign saying "Put Walter In."*

"Somebody's telling you how to coach when you've been coaching for 22 years and the most athletic thing they've ever done is jump to a conclusion."

> *George Raveling, on some fans*

"Fans never fall asleep at our games, because they're afraid they might get hit by a pass."

> *George Raveling*

"They were booing me at the baggage claim. That's a record."

> *Rony Seikaly, on being hated by*
> *Charlotte fans*

FIGHT TO THE FINISH

"I want to be registered as a lethal weapon."

> *Charles Barkley, asked why he was*
> *studying karate*

"I threw a left hand, but I was backpedaling so fast it never got there."

> *Bob Ferry, on a fight with Wilt Chamberlain*

"He'll have to run down to the end of the bench, chasing a loose ball, to get to me."

> *Scott Hastings, after Charles Barkley said "I owe you one" for an earlier fight they had*

"For $58,000, I'd have liked to have hit him more than once."

> *Michael Jordan, on being fined $58,000 for an altercation with Reggie Miller*

"If a guy takes off his wristwatch before he fights, he means business."

> *Al McGuire*

"My theory on fighting is don't fight fair. Surprise 'em. Get 'em when they're coming out of church."

> *Calvin Murphy*

"He must have thought my head was a Bahamian conga drum, It felt good. I thought it was a scalp massage."

Mychal Thompson, after Isiah Thomas was thrown out of a game for slapping Thompson on the head

FINAL FOUR

"The more Final Fours you go to, the more cousins you find you have who need tickets."
Mike Krzyzewski

"Thank God it wasn't [*starting center Darrel*] Imhoff."

Pete Newell, former California coach, after hearing his wife broke her hand before the Final Four

"The Final Four is so much bull anymore. It's shoe salesmen and nine-man coaching staffs and plastic men in three-piece suits. It's a circus. It's a carnival . . . It's still the King of the Hill."

Dave Pritchett, assistant coach at Oral Roberts

"I'm going to name my next child Al B. Querque."
>*Jim Valvano, after North Carolina State won the NCAA Championship in Albuquerque*

"Why shouldn't I milk it? We're an agricultural institution."
>*Jim Valvano, on getting lots of endorsement offers after North Carolina State's championship*

FINES AND SUSPENSIONS

"Because I hang around with Rick Mahorn. I'm guilty by association."
>*Charles Barkley, on why he is fined so much*

"We were going to donate the money to the homeless, but they would have better houses than us by the end of the season."
>*Charles Barkley, on he and Rick Mahorn donating their fines to the homeless*

"I told him for $250 he could buy a heck of an alarm clock."

> *Dan Issel, on fining Brian Williams*
> *$250 for oversleeping*

"All it means is my wife will get a potted plant instead of a diamond necklace for our anniversary in August."

> *Bill Laimbeer, on being fined $5,000*

"I understand they are calling Charles Barkley 'The Bridge' because of all his suspensions."

> *Glenn Liebman, sportswriter*

"Throwing Mark Price out of a basketball game is like throwing the pope out of the Vatican."

> *Paul Mokeski, on the clean-cut Price*
> *being thrown out of a game*

"We took a vote as to what he might have said, whether it was 'golly' or 'gosh.'"

> *Randy Pfund, on A. C. Green, an*
> *ordained minister, being thrown out*
> *of a game*

"It's fair to say that when it comes to visits to my office, Charles is in a class by himself."

Rod Thorn, NBA VP in charge of suspensions and fines

FIRING LINE

"If you see me hanging, cut me down before you go out and play."

Bill Fitch, on constant rumors about his being fired as Nets coach

"I guess I must have rated between 2 and 5."

Mike Fratello, on Atlanta management calling him one of the five best coaches in the NBA shortly before firing him

"I took the liberty of firing myself before anyone else did."

Jim Klein, coach of Utica (CBA), on resigning after a 2–12 start

"Not at all, but I plan to buy a glass-bottomed car so I can watch the look on his face when I run over him."

> *Abe Lemons, asked if he was mad at DeLoss Dodds, Texas athletic director, after being fired*

"I looked around the room and nobody else was there, so he had to be talking to me."

> *Abe Lemons, on being fired by Dodds*

"What am I going to do with all the orange clothes I bought?"

> *Abe Lemons, on being fired as Texas coach*

"I told some former players not to throw gum on the floor because I might be the one that would have to pick it up."

> *Shelby Metcalf, on being told he would be reassigned after being fired as Texas A&M coach*

"When you're hired, you're fired. The date just hasn't been put in."

> *C. M. Newton*

"It ended so quickly, I didn't even get a chance to ride on the team charter."

> *Lois Tarkanian, on her husband Jerry being fired early in his coaching stint with the San Antonio Spurs*

FLASHBACKS

"I have flashbacks all the time, but none are related to basketball."

> *Kurt Rambis, asked if Sacramento winning two games in a row brought flashbacks to his days with the Lakers*

FOOD FOR THOUGHT

"My cholesterol level went down 30 percent when I was recruiting him."

> *Kevin Bannon, Trenton State coach, on recruiting a player who spent his summer working at a seafood restaurant*

"That's my next move. I'm going to have my own salad dressing."

> *Charles Barkley, on being as popular in Japan as Paul Newman*

"To sell nachos in the concession stand. We're making a bundle off those things."

> *Doug Barnes, coach at University of Arkansas–Monticello, on his best coaching decision of the year*

"They brought us crayfish on steroids."

> *Jason Bossard, Michigan player, on huge shrimp served to him during a tournament in Milan*

"I'm just a caraway seed in the bakery of life."
> *Pete Gillen*

"Saltwater taffy."

> *Caldwell Jones, asked to name his favorite seafood*

"All of them."

> *Darryl Kennedy, Oklahoma player, asked to name his favorite food*

"Yeah, they were delicious."

Frank Layden, on being sent flowers
by Pat Williams after being named
Coach of the Year

"When I got home after practice one night, my young wife met me at the door crying, 'Darling, the dog ate the meat loaf I made for you.' . . . I took her in my arms and said, 'Stop crying, honey, I'll buy you another dog.'"

Abe Lemons

"Thank God. They electrocuted the chef."

Abe Lemons, on lights going out
during a banquet

"Zone Xavier and get something to eat."

Abe Lemons, on strategy he had for
playing Xavier

"Win or lose, I eat my ass off."

Rick Majerus, asked how he reacts to
a tough loss

"I used to be to vegetables what Orson Welles was to pole vaulting."

Rick Majerus, on losing 100 pounds

"For a while I was eating so many oats, I started counting with my foot."

Rick Majerus, on dieting after heart surgery

"He only eats one meal a day. Unfortunately, it lasts all day."

Mack McCarthy, Auburn assistant coach, on Charles Barkley in his college days

"If the waitress has dirty ankles, the chili should be good."

Al McGuire

"I like airline food."

Melvin Turpin, after telling the media he weighed 265 pounds and then flying to Cleveland the next day and weighing in at 282 pounds

"You can't get cooking in more than two minutes. I'm not a microwaver. I'm a steady oven. Let me out there and you'll have a nice dinner."

> *Rex Walters, on averaging only two minutes a game*

FOOTBALL

"I want to be the hitter, not the hittee."

> *Charles Barkley, on why he would like to be a professional linebacker*

"The football team outscored us."

> *Dave Bliss, on his days of coaching an anemic offensive Oklahoma team*

"I think basketball would be his first love simply because he can live longer."

> *Bobby Bowden, on why Charlie Ward chose professional basketball over football*

"If I was going to get beat up, I wanted it to be indoors where it was warm."

Tom Heinsohn, on why he chose
professional basketball over football

"They're all going to the NBA."

Chuck Knox, football coach, on why
there are no great tight ends in the
NFL

"I'd rather be a football coach. That way you only lose 11 games a year."

Abe Lemons

"They do one-armed push-ups so they can count with the other hand."

Al McGuire, on football players

"When I went to Catholic High School in Philadelphia, we just had one coach for football and basketball. He took all of us who turned out and had us run through a forest. The ones who ran into the trees were on the football team."

George Raveling

"It's somebody who loves his wife more than football."

> *Sonny Smith, former Auburn*
> *basketball coach, asked his definition*
> *of an Alabama pervert*

FOULS

"It got so bad for me I'd foul, just go to hacking to avoid the trillion."

> *Scott Hastings, on avoiding the*
> *dreaded trillion—0 field goals, 0 free*
> *throws, 00 rebounds (offensive and*
> *defensive), 0 assists, 0 personal fouls,*
> *and 0 total points*

"If a 17-year-old shoots somebody, you don't go out and arrest the mother."

> *Frank Layden, on the stupidity of the*
> *NBA rule calling for the suspension*
> *of a coach if a player commits a*
> *flagrant foul*

"I'm calling myself Desert. No food, no water, no calls."

> *Shaquille O'Neal*

"I told him it looked like he was auditioning for a job at Benihana—chop, chop, chop. At this rate, he'll be head chef."

> *Robert Parish, on tutoring Acie Earl, who had a proclivity for getting into foul trouble*

"They called fouls like they were getting a commission."

> *Peter Salzberg, University of Vermont coach, after his team was assessed a high number of fouls*

"You want to know the theory people play with today? Coaches tell the kids, 'All five of you guys go ahead and foul at once, because they can only call one of 'em.'"

> *Sonny Smith*

"If you showed the game to Hulk Hogan, he wouldn't want to come here."

> *Bob Weltlick, former Texas basketball coach, on the tough play and many fouls in a Texas-SMU game*

FREE AGENTS

"You haven't been a professional athlete unless you've had a cortisone shot and been a free agent."

> *Rich Kelley, on why he declared for free agency*

FREE THROWS

"We defend against the free throw very well."

> *Lyle Damon, San Francisco State basketball coach, on opponents shooting 57 percent from the line against them*

"It ties the school record for highest free-throw percentage in a game."

> *John Justus, Wake Forest sports information director, putting a positive spin on Wake Forest shooting only 1-for-1 from the free-throw line for an entire game*

"I'm trying my hardest, but I can't have everything. I can't have the looks, the rapping ability, the scoring ability, and the free throws."

> *Shaquille O'Neal, on being a poor foul shooter*

"We're shooting 100 percent—60 percent from the field and 40 percent from the free-throw line."

> *Norm Stewart, Missouri coach*

"It's one thing to hear about it from your coach, but when your wife tells you it stinks, you tend to work on it."

> *Orlando Woolridge, on his poor free-throw shooting*

FUN TO STAY AT THE YMCA

"We did have three go to the YMCA."

> *Abe Lemons, asked if any of his players made it to the NBA*

"Nothing means nothing. But it isn't really nothing, because nothing is something that isn't."
Darryl Dawkins

"You said practice was ten to eleven, and that's what time it is now."
Marc Ivaroni, explaining to his coach why he showed up for practice at 10:50

"It's really great being Magic Johnson the basketball player for eight months and just plain Earvin Johnson the other three."
Magic Johnson

"Now that I'm here—we'll turn this program around 360 degrees."
Jason Kidd, after being drafted second by the Mavericks

"The Sonics are 19–0 in games they lead after the fourth quarter."
Rick Moxley, Supersonics PR director

"I figured at this point in the season we'd be .500."
Jim Valvano, after North Carolina
State was off to a 5–0 start

FUNDAMENTALS

"I don't believe in boxing out. My idea about rebounding is just to go get the damned ball."
Charles Barkley

"He couldn't play for us. He's too fundamentally sound. We wouldn't have a damn thing to talk about at halftime."
Benny Dees, New Orleans coach, on
Colorado State center Eric Friehauf

"The lack of hustle and thinking bothers me on some pro teams. Heck, if I want to watch great individuals play, I'll watch golf or track."
John Wooden

THE FUTURE

"Most of our future lies ahead."
   Denny Crum

"If I could look into the future, I wouldn't be
sitting here talking to you doorknobs; I'd be out
investing in the stock market."
   *Kevin McHale, asked by reporters
   about the Celtics' future*

"Mainly, because I got a pension coming."
   *Bill Russell, on why he worries about
   the NBA's future*

GAMBLIN' MAN

"It's close to Las Vegas."
   *Michael Jordan, asked what he likes
   about playing in Utah*

"I would quit, buy the team [Cleveland], and move it to Las Vegas. And I'd make sure the arena had slot machines next to them so I could get a cut of the action."

> *Paul Mokeski, asked what he would do if he won $35 million in the Ohio lottery*

"The security guys called me over and told me I wouldn't be bothered by the media. They welcomed me with big smiles. I thought they liked me. Then I figured out it was $25,000 a hand."

> *Shaquille O'Neal, on his first visit to Caesar's Palace*

"No doubt about it, it's Las Vegas. You lose the game and you lose your money."

> *Bobby Paschal, South Florida basketball coach, asked what is the worst place to play*

"It's like the old story my dad told me. When you go to a card game and look around for the suckers at the table, if you don't find one, it's probably you."

> *Charles Spoonhour, St. Louis coach, on competition at the Great Midwest Classic*

"The game plan was for me to score the first 212, but I got tired."

> *Kevin McHale, on scoring 11 points in the first two and a half minutes of a game*

"Sometimes we get out there and say, 'Oh, this is what we're supposed to do.' Even if the guy fell down with a heart attack, we'd still throw him the ball."

> *Kevin McHale, on the structured Celtics offense*

GATORADE

"I'd have to have two Gatorades going at the end of the bench. One would be regular, the other decaf."

> *Tim Capstraw, Wagner coach, on the possibility of playing in a tournament game at 9 A.M.*

"Coaches get fired every day, but a GM can be dumb and last forever."

Doug Moe

"He was absolutely depressed. I wanted to fly him up here [Orlando] and burp him. He really needed a shoulder to cry on."

Pat Williams, on John Nash, the 76ers GM, being disconsolate during a long losing streak

"It's like a nervous breakdown with a weekly paycheck."

Pat Williams, describing the job of general manager

"He signed me to a multiday contract."

Pat Williams, on his tenuous relationship with 76ers owner Harold Katz

"How big is the hole we're in? You're in the right state for big holes. We fit right into the Grand Canyon."

> *Charles Barkley, describing the hole Phoenix was in being down two games to none to Chicago during the 1993 NBA finals*

"I would have been a great Pilgrim. . . . I would have steered that ship [the Mayflower] to the right place. . . . I probably would have skipped America and set sail straight for Hawaii."

> *Darryl Dawkins*

"I knew that I would be going places, and I just wanted to know where I was when I got there."

> *Michael Jordan, on majoring in geography in college*

"None of us guys like the city of Utah."

> *Vernon Maxwell, on playing the Jazz*

"I won't say it's remote up here, but my last speech was reviewed in *Field and Stream*."

George Raveling, on coaching at Washington State

"I'd rather be in jail in Sacramento than be the mayor of Boston."

Bill Russell

"I don't get to play. The team stinks. My wife lives in Denver. And it's been twenty below all season."

Danny Schayes, asked his opinion about playing in Milwaukee

"I told them not to worry about it, since we were going to play indoors."

Jerry Tarkanian, on preparing his players for the high elevation in Wyoming

GLOBETROTTERS

"I'm looking forward to you passing the ball around here, but please take it easy. We only rent."

> *President Gerald Ford, to the Harlem Globetrotters, on visiting the White House*

"I think only the Harlem Globetrotters and Washington Generals play each other that much."

> *Rene Portland, Penn State women's coach, on playing Rutgers five times during the season*

GOD BLESS TEXAS

"I hope they [his enemies] notice the mistletoe tied to my coattails as I leave town."

> *Abe Lemons, on moving from Texas to Oklahoma State*

"It's the only place that I ever got offered a job where they had a school song."

> *Abe Lemons, on why he took the coaching job at the University of Texas*

"Couldn't even win the scrimmage."

> *Abe Lemons, on his Texas team scrimmaging against each other at halftime*

"We got to see all of Hearne, and parts of His'n."

> *Shelby Metcalf, on his team being stranded in the town of Hearne*

GOLF

"They told me I'd have time to work on my game here. I didn't know they meant my golf game."

> *Steve Kerr, on averaging less than 10 minutes a game for Orlando*

"I look at a golf course as a great waste of pastureland."

> *Karl Malone, on his job as a cattle farmer*

"When I was growing up, my mother wouldn't allow me near a golf course. She didn't think the people were very nice. Now I play every day, and you know what? She was right."

> *Bill Russell*

GUARDS

"Some guards are so small, they're looking through the knees, and if they're not looking through a bowlegged guy, you don't see what's going on on the other side of the court."

> *Bill Fitch*

"I can't run my fingers through my hair."

> *Kareem Abdul-Jabbar, asked if there*
> *was anything he couldn't do after 15*
> *years in the NBA*

"I got in a bad accident and broke all my hairs."

> *Darryl Dawkins, on his shaved head*

"Hearing the crowd was great. It made what little hair I had stand on end."

> *Alex English, on receiving a standing*
> *ovation after scoring 54 points*

"My image was mature, so people expected me to be that. I'm not panicking, like you guys, about being 30 and my hair turning gray. I lost my hair three years ago."

> *Michael Jordan, to a group of*
> *sportswriters, on turning 30*

"With Michael, you just hope and pray a lot. You go to church and you try to talk about things Michael doesn't like to talk about, like baldness."
John Salley, on Michael Jordan

HAKEEM THE DREAM

"You go into the paint against him and he'll mess up your digestive tract. You'll be puking leather for two days."
Shelby Metcalf, on facing Hakeem Olajuwon in college

HALFTIME

"Baryshnikov was booked. So we went with Barry."
Stan Kasten, on booking Dancing Barry for a halftime show

"I've heard my halftime talks and they aren't much."
Abe Lemons, asked if his halftime talks inspired any victories

"If that guy makes a turnover, we're gonna be in deep trouble."

> *Rick Sund, Mavericks official, on a halftime show featuring a man who juggles chain saws*

MARV HARSHMAN

"I tried to find a Christmas present for Marv, but what do you give the guy who has nothing?"
> *George Raveling, on the former Washington coach*

HARVARD

"If I ask a kid how he did on the boards, and he says, 'Twelve a game,' I know he's not going to Harvard."
> *Peter Roby, Harvard coach*

"Monday through Friday they want you to be like Harvard. On Saturday, they want you to play like Oklahoma."

> *Jim Valvano, on coaching at North Carolina State*

THE HAWK

"The Hawk is a work of art. Some nights, he's poetry in motion; other nights, still life."

> *Joe Gilmartin, on Connie Hawkins*

HAWKS

"The Hawks won't win because the NBA won't allow you to play with more than one basketball."

> *Charles Barkley, on the offensive-minded Atlanta Hawks*

"We're going to be exciting. Of course, it was exciting when the *Titanic* went down."

> *Bob Weiss, on the Hawks' prospects in 1992*

HEAT

"I'm scared. I think I'm the best player here."
Scott Hastings, on the first year of the expansion Miami Heat

"I am planning to stay positive, even though some negativity is creeping into this team like gangrene in a wound."
John Salley, on the Heat

HEIGHT REPORT

"I can't miss a class. The professor doesn't have to call the roll to know I'm not there."
Tom Burleson, 7'4", on his days at North Carolina State

"I believe in higher education. You know, 6'8", 6'9", 6'10"."
David "Smokey" Gaines, San Diego State coach

"No, I clean giraffe ears."

> *Elvin Hayes, asked if he was a*
> *basketball player*

"If you go to the movies with him, you get in for half price."

> *Johnny Kerr, on the 7'2" Mark Eaton*

"No, ma'am, I'm a jockey for a dinosaur."

> *Johnny Kerr, asked if he played*
> *basketball*

"I didn't like being tall when I was little."

> *Eric Montross*

"When he sits down, his ears pop."

> *Don Nelson, on 7'7" Shawn Bradley*

"People will look up at me and say, 'Oh, my God.' I'll tell 'em, 'No, I'm your center.'"

> *Chuck Nevitt, on being 7'5"*

"I never worried about being adopted."

Chuck Nevitt, on having two brothers who were 6'7", a father who was 6'7", and a 6-foot-tall mother

"He was born on June 6th, 7th, and 8th."

George Raveling, on the 7'2" James Donaldson

"I'm not on a ladder."

Willis Reed, told by the Knicks publicist to be careful not to fall off the ladder while painting

"When you don't have height, it's like taking a BB gun on a safari."

Bob Reinhart, Georgia State coach, after being beaten soundly by Georgia Tech

"Because that's where the basket is."

Spud Webb, 5'7", asked why he likes to drive the lane against taller players

HOCKEY

"What are you going to call the Bruins—the Cuddly Bears?"

> *Kevin McHale, on hearing that the new Anaheim NHL expansion team was named the Mighty Ducks*

"I like all sports, and I like to play them all—except ice hockey."

> *Shaquille O'Neal*

"Basketball is the one sport that can truly be influenced by one man. Baseball and football can't, and hockey no one understands anyway."

> *Pat Williams*

HOMETOWN

"It was so small, we didn't have a village idiot. My brother and I had to take turns."

> *Dick Motta, on his hometown of Union, Utah*

HOT ROD HUNDLEY

"He's the most overrated player since myself."
*Hot Rod Hundley, on Ralph
Sampson*

"We could fill the Salt Palace if we just invited the
people Hot Rod owes drinks to."
Frank Layden

HUMAN HIGHLIGHT FILM

"That's the one with all the No Passing signs."
*An Atlanta DJ, joking about a
highway named after Dominique
Wilkins*

"Me trying to guard Dominique is like me trying
to speak French or Italian."
*Horace Grant, on trying to guard
Dominique Wilkins*

HUNTING

"I'm not going hunting with anyone who plays the same position as me."

> *Derrick Coleman, on why he*
> *wouldn't go hunting with teammate*
> *Jayson Williams*

"I gave up hunting and fishing for this."

> *Bill Fitch, after the Nets lost a game*
> *by almost 40 points*

ICE MAN COMETH

"I'd steal his car so he couldn't go to the arena. I might get arrested, but I wouldn't be embarrassed."

> *Bill Russell, on the best way to*
> *defend against George "Ice Man"*
> *Gervin*

INJURY REPORT

"He's incredible. If you drop a toothpick on his foot, he'll have a stress fracture."
Stan Albeck, on Bill Walton

"I've never had knee surgery before on any other part of my body."
Winston Bennett

"It's not bad. Now I can park in the handicapped zones without feeling guilty."
Larry Bird, on having casts on both feet

"The team picture is an x-ray."
John Cirillo, Knicks publicist, during an injury-plagued Knicks season

"What I need is a six-leaf clover."
Ken Conley, Oklahoma center, on suffering from chicken pox, a knee injury, and a broken finger in the same season

113

"We never had pulled groins when I played, and we had groins."

Bob Ferry, on a plethora of pulled groins in the NBA

"I called Blue Cross, but they hung up when they found out who it was."

Bill Fitch, on an injury-decimated Cavaliers team

"My body could stand the crutches, but my mind couldn't stand the sidelines."

Michael Jordan, on missing 64 games in the 1985–86 season

"Damn, that's the same one I broke a couple of years ago."

Joe C. Meriweather, on breaking his nose

"I think they should send me to the Bahamas. I hear salt water is good for tendinitis."

Paul Mokeski

"I want to be a stress fracture. No one understands what it is, so they respect you and leave you alone."

Dick Motta, on what he wants to be in his next life

"It was the same right foot that Scottie Pippen injured a year ago."

Ahmad Rashad

"My players say I taped the ankles as well as I coach. I don't think it was a compliment."

Jerry Reynolds, on taping up players while the trainer was sick

"We've had such bad luck with injuries. I even broke my wrist playing tennis over the summer. Of course, most people in Sacramento would consider that good luck."

Jerry Reynolds

"At this rate, Pervis is going to be a great player for my successor."

Jerry Reynolds, on Pervis Ellison playing only 25 minutes in his first 10 games for Sacramento

"I was pretty sure I didn't have a heart attack, but I knew it wasn't a normal way to leave. I was the first one out of the parking lot, though."

> *Jerry Reynolds, after fainting on the sidelines and being rushed to the hospital*

"It's like the other heel in Panama—very irritating, and it won't go away."

> *Mychal Thompson, on comparing his heel fracture to Panamanian dictator Manuel Noriega*

"I learned a long time ago that minor surgery is when they do the operation on someone else, not you."

> *Bill Walton*

"He's going to get their Medicaid rate up."

> *Lenny Wilkens, asked for his reaction to the Clippers acquiring Bill Walton*

"I'm a basketball player, not a monk. I play the women, I play the cars, I play everything I can. I'm 22, and a 22-year-old kid ain't no genius."
Marvin Barnes

"John made a 32 on his ACT. That's unbelievable. I could take it six times and add them all up, and it wouldn't come to 32."
Dale Brown, on recruit John Tudor

"To use the word 'genius' about a basketball coach is ridiculous. A genius is a Beethoven, a Mozart, the Beatles."
Pete Carril, Princeton coach, on being hailed as a genius

"My intelligence is at times baffling. . . . If people ain't prepared for me, they may walk away knowing less than they did when they walked up."
Edgar Jones

"On the line where 'church preference' was requested, the guy wrote 'red brick.'"

> *Frank Layden, on one of Layden's*
> *players filling out an application*

"It was awful. Everybody knew I was the dumbest one in the room."

> *Frank Layden, on giving a speech at*
> *Harvard Law School*

"I told him, 'Son, I can't understand it with you. Is it ignorance or apathy?' He said, 'Coach, I don't know and I don't care.'"

> *Frank Layden, on one of his players*

"You could tell five guys to go over to the post office at two o'clock and one of them wouldn't be there. So why have so many tricky plays?"

> *Abe Lemons*

"We don't exactly have Phi Beta Kappas in this league."

> *Nancy Lieberman, on the difficulties*
> *of learning the plays after joining the*
> *United States Basketball League*

"That guy is so lucky. He'd call me on the phone, he'd flip the coin, and I'd call it. He won every single time."

> *Shelby Metcalf, Texas A&M coach, on always losing the coin toss in a tournament to Houston coach Guy Lewis*

"He once asked me if Beirut was named after the famous baseball player who hit home runs."

> *Brother Ray Page, St. Anthony's (Jersey City, NJ) high school teacher, on Bobby Hurley*

"I asked him to spell Mississippi. He said, 'The state or the river?'"

> *George Raveling, on one of his recruits*

"The blood couldn't make it to my little brain."

> *Jerry Reynolds, on why he passed out on the sidelines while coaching*

"I wasn't very smart when I was growing up. When the teacher started talking about Sherlock Holmes, I thought it was a housing development."

> *Sonny Smith*

"He's a quick learner, but he forgets quick too."
Mychal Thompson, on Yugoslavian
import Vlade Divac

"We have a very intelligent team. I've had clubs that when you tell a guy to go back door, he leaves the gym. Or you tell the team you're going to have a closed practice and eight guys don't show up."
Jim Valvano

ALLEN IVERSON

"I've been through three calf shows, nine horse ropings, and I saw Elvis once, but I've never seen anything like that Iverson boy."
Nolan Richardson, on Allen Iverson

"They talk about transition from offense to defense in basketball. I had to make one from Bourbon Street to here."

> *Hot Rod Hundley, Jazz announcer,*
> *on moving from New Orleans to Utah*

"Time was when admitting to be the Jazz coach was like saying you were the lookout at Pearl Harbor."

> *Frank Layden*

"We're America's team. But nobody knows it."

> *Frank Layden, on the anonymity of*
> *the Jazz*

"I'm from Brooklyn. I rooted for the Dodgers. I believe in miracles."

> *Frank Layden, on Utah's long-shot*
> *playoff chances*

"I'm not going to have my feelings hurt if the Jazz don't want to make me their vice president. All I want is free tickets."

> *Karl Malone, on retirement plans*

JOB SECURITY

"When you're kicked upstairs, make sure you're not working in a one-story building."
Johnny Kerr

"When I was at Auburn, they bought Pat Dye [the Auburn football coach] a $400,000 house and an annuity. They bought me a mobile home and told me not to take the wheels off."
Sonny Smith

MICHAEL JORDAN

"Picture Duke Ellington while playing the piano discovering he has a gift for the slide trombone."
David Aldridge, Washington Post *reporter, on Jordan's newfound greatness from three-point range*

"Take security, but just go out. Or be like me, just punch a few people, give them $10,000. Michael can afford it."

> *Charles Barkley, on his belief that*
> *Jordan should derive more enjoyment*
> *from his celebrity status*

"On a scale of one to ten, with the rest of the superstars an eight, he's a ten. . . . I just hope there aren't any more of him to come along that we have to deal with."

> *Larry Bird*

"He's tenacious, sagacious, vivacious, and hellacious."

> *Walt Frazier, on Jordan*

"I'm often mentioned in the same sentence as Michael Jordan: 'You know that Scott Hastings; he's no Michael Jordan.'"

> *Scott Hastings*

"Never got the chance. I always fouled him."

> *Scott Hastings, after calling Jordan's*
> *never dunking on him his greatest*
> *career accomplishment*

"You don't bring your wife and children to the game when he comes to town, 'cause he'll embarrass you."

Mark Jackson

"It's nice just to play against him. Sometimes you get your picture in the paper."

Eddie Johnson

"If he doesn't want to be an ambassador, then tell him to stop scoring 30 points a game. Tell him to stop winning."

Larry Johnson, on Jordan's statements that he didn't want to be an ambassador for basketball

"I take that as a personal insult. I can hold him to 65 on any given night."

Steve Kerr, on Jordan saying he could score 70 to 80 points against Cleveland with starting guard Craig Ehlo hurt

"We were playing and Michael dunked on me. I felt real bad until I saw him dance."

Kid, actor and dancer who had several successful movies with his partner Play, discussing Jordan's MTV video

"I'll always remember this as the night that Michael Jordan and I combined to score 70 points."

Stacey King, after scoring one point on a day Jordan had 69

"Why do you even want to talk about it? Let a dead horse sleep."

Alton Lister, on the success Golden State had against Jordan

"Every time he dunks, you know you could wind up on one of his posters. Man, he makes me glad I'm retired."

Billy McKinney

"I am telling you, he's not human. Has anyone ever seen him bleed? I have not seen blood yet. Something is going on here. He is not human."

Reggie Miller

"The only man who consistently held Michael Jordan to fewer than 20 points a game."

C. W. Nevius, San Francisco
Chronicle *writer, on Dean Smith,*
Jordan's college coach

"Magic is the best player who plays on the ground, and Michael is the best player who plays in the air."

John Paxson

"In my prime I could have handled Michael Jordan. Of course, he would be only 12 years old."

Jerry Sloan

"You don't hesitate with Michael, or you'll end up on some poster in a gift shop someplace."

Felton Spencer

"I think he is some kind of alien. I think he was kidnapped and brought back here, some kind of ET thing."

Donnie Walsh

"Offense and defense."
> *Bob Weiss, on being asked where the*
> *Bulls would miss Jordan the most*

"It's like being on tour with the Jacksons. He's Michael and we're the Jacksons."
> *Orlando Woolridge, on being one of*
> *Jordan's supporting cast*

JUMP BALL

"This will be the first time the referee drops the ball."
> *Dan Issel, anticipating a jump ball*
> *between Michael Adams and Muggsy*
> *Bogues*

"Considering their leaping ability, a face-off would have been more appropriate."
> *Paul Westphal, on a jump ball*
> *between Ed Nealy and Scott Hastings*

"Hey, Rick, that's the first time I ever saw you shake a hand from Kentucky that doesn't have money in it."

> *Larry Bird, on Rick Robey shaking hands with Kentucky coach Joe B. Hall*

"They're great. We could play them ten times and lose nine and I wouldn't be sure we'd win the tenth."

> *Rick Majerus*

"They used to call what we played 'ghetto ball.' Now guys like Rick Pitino play the same kind of game at Kentucky and it's called up-tempo. I guess it's in style."

> *Nolan Richardson, on Arkansas's "forty minutes of hell" philosophy*

"Kentucky players put their pants on the same way our players do. It just takes them a little longer to pull them up."

> *Joe Sexson, Butler coach*

KINGS

"You have to be around the Kings any length of time. Either that or a blithering idiot."

Jerry Reynolds, on being the world's greatest optimist

KISS AND TELL

"That was the first time I've ever been kissed by anybody who was cut."

Jack McCloskey, on Ann Meyers having a tryout with the Pacers in 1979

"I liked it better when we hated Philly and we hated L.A. Now everybody has the same agent and they all hug and kiss after the game."

Kevin McHale

"If I went out and tried to kiss Willis Reed before one of our games, I'd be picking up my teeth. And Willis and I are friends."

> *Wes Unseld, on Magi. Johnson and Isiah Thomas kissing each other before playoff games*

"That's the first time a client ever kissed me good-bye."

> *Bob Woolf, agent of Carol Blazejowski, who signed a big contract with the Women's Pro Basketball League*

BOBBY KNIGHT

"Please, I've got one more game to play."

> *Steve Alford, asked to discuss Knight before the 1987 NCAA finals*

"Very well. I just do everything he tells me."

> *Lee Corso, Indiana football coach, asked how he gets along with Knight*

"I wish he'd decide which I was so I know what to wear."

John Feinstein, on Bobby Knight
calling him a pimp and a whore for
writing A Season on the Brink

"It's strange Bobby was the worst defensive player on the team, yet his teams now are so defense oriented."

John Havlicek, a teammate of Knight
at Ohio State

"If the NBA were on channel 5 and a bunch of frogs making love was on channel 4, I'd watch the frogs even if they were coming in fuzzy."

Bobby Knight

"It's a chance to do something for your country without killing anybody."

George Raveling, on agreeing to be
an assistant coach to Knight for the
'84 U.S. Olympic team

"Bobby Knight has three new phones in his house so he can hang up on more sportswriters."

George Raveling

"He's the kind of guy who would throw a beer party and then lock the bathroom door on you."
George Raveling

"Bobby is a good friend of mine. But if I ever need a heart transplant, I want his. It's never been used."
George Raveling

"I'd like to say I'm not Bobby Knight, but I can work on my profanity."
Jerry Reynolds, while being introduced as the Kings' head coach

"He coaches basketball like a football coach—not wishy-washy like some basketball coaches I've known."
Bo Schembechler

"That's like going from General Patton to Gomer Pyle."
Dick Vitale, on the possibility of a player transferring from Indiana to North Carolina State

CHRISTIAN LAETTNER

"We're a lot alike actually. We both attended great academic institutions. And when we walk into a room, women scream."

> *Charles Barkley, comparing himself to Laettner*

"I think he will eventually have the credentials to back up everything he thinks about himself."
> *Jack McCloskey*

BILL LAIMBEER

"Of all the guys I've bumped heads and traded elbows with during my NBA career, I thought Bill Laimbeer was the whiniest, the most despicable, the most disgusting guy in the game. On the other hand, I've always respected him as a player."
> *Charles Barkley*

"Kevin's a little dude and it doesn't take much to knock him down."

Charles Barkley, after Bill Laimbeer
knocked down Kevin Johnson

"If Mother Teresa played in the NBA, after one encounter with Laimbeer, she'd want to fight."

Jan Hubbard, Newsday *sportswriter*

"I'm glad we didn't play together. I'd hate to have any reason to like him."

John Paxson, on attending Notre
Dame after Laimbeer left

"I'm sorry Isiah is not going to be playing. But in my opinion, he couldn't have picked a better guy to punch."

Scott Skiles, on Isiah Thomas missing
a game after getting into a fight with
Laimbeer

"I knew I made the team when I came out of the shower and Laimbeer said hello to me. It's the first time he'd said anything to me in training camp."

Charles Thomas

"The Lakers are so good they could have a fast break with a medicine ball."

> *Rich Donnelly, on the Magic/Kareem era*

"I'd have booed too. I looked up in the stands and I thought I saw my wife and kids booing."

> *Jerry Reynolds, after the Kings lost badly to the Lakers*

"We're a lot more comfortable breathing the air we can see."

> *Mychal Thompson, on why the Lakers play well at home*

"I felt like a condemned man sitting in the electric chair and just before they were ready to pull the switch, not only do I get my sentence commuted, but I get clemency, a pardon, and they put me up in the best hotel free of charge."

> *Mychal Thompson, on being traded from the Spurs to the Lakers*

LAND DOWN UNDER

"Tell him to get a 6'10" father and a 6'4" mother and head to America as quickly as possible."
> *Luc Longley, offering advice to friends in his home country of Australia*

"What else would you expect on a kangaroo court?"
> *Allan Malamud, Los Angeles Times columnist, on the Australian national team being unbeaten*

LANGUAGE

"The first phrase I want to learn is 'give me the ball.' The second is 'get out of the way.' The rest will take care of itself."
> *Rolando Blackman, on playing for a team in Greece*

"I'm not stupid. I just talk stupid."
> *Lefty Driesell, on claims that he's stupid*

"Not only did we lose but we were defeated in four different languages."

Ron Krayl, Monmouth coach, on losing to Marist, who had several players from foreign countries

"It may throw me off course but never off curse."

Kevin Loughery, on a ruling that forces coaches to remain in a smaller area of the sidelines

"Talk doesn't hurt you. Talk is just a figure of speech."

Charles Oakley

"I'll never forget one of his pep talks, before a Laker game. There were 72 bleeps in it and it was Christmas day."

Paul Westphal, on Tommy Heinsohn

FRANK LAYDEN

"When the list of great coaches is finally read—I believe Frank Layden will be there listening."

Pat Williams, at a roast for Layden

"Even though he lived by the beach in college, he didn't have a tan. Now, that's a serious player."

> *Bill Fitch, on Connor Henry from the*
> *University of California at Santa*
> *Barbara*

"At Detroit, we gave kids room, board, and a shotgun. Here, we give them room, board, and a surfboard."

> *Dave "Smokey" Gaines, on the*
> *contrast between the University of*
> *Detroit and San Diego State*

"The position of UCLA and USC in athletics is like the Arabs in oil. By a quirk of nature, they're sitting on 50 percent of the world's supply."

> *George Raveling*

"Sacramento is not in California."

> *Reggie Theus, asked, after being*
> *traded to the Kings, how it felt being*
> *back in his home state*

"I guess there's not a lot of sun in gyms."

> *Kiki Vandeweghe, on not having a*
> *tan even though he played for UCLA*

LEGENDS GAME

"Where's the beer?"

> *Hot Rod Hundley, after hitting an*
> *amazing 15-foot hook shot in a 1993*
> *Legends game*

"I stood up and yelled at my wife all week."

> *Johnny Kerr, on how he prepared for*
> *coaching a basketball Legends game*

"I'm going to sell them 48-minute term insurance."

> *Johnny Kerr, a former insurance*
> *salesman, asked what kind of*
> *insurance players in a Legends game*
> *needed*

"My son said as soon as I get in the game, I should foul somebody to prove I played."

> *George Yardley, on playing in a*
> *Legends game*

LOOK BEFORE YOU LEAP

"I've guarded other guys who could leap high before. But all of them came down."

> *Bob Hansen, on guarding Darrell Griffith*

LOSING

"Show me a good loser and I'll show you a loser."

> *Red Auerbach*

"It was the most difficult year I've had since puberty."

> *Dave Bliss, SMU coach, on a 7–20 record*

"The taste of defeat has a richness of experience all its own."

> *Bill Bradley*

"I dreamed I'd have a heart attack and die and the obituary would read, 'The only NBA coach who never won a game.'"

> *Don Casey, Clippers coach, on winning a game after losing his first 19 as coach*

"It was so bad, my travel agent called me with a play—and I wrote it down."

> *Benny Dees, on a bad slump during his days as coach of Wyoming*

"I've never been to a mercy killing before."

> *Benny Dees, New Orleans coach, on losing by 25 points to Alabama*

"We're the only team in history that could lose nine games in a row and then go into a slump."

> *Bill Fitch, on a bad Cavaliers team*

"Last year we weren't all that bad. We led the league in flu shots."

> *Bill Fitch, on the same team*

"If we had a bad season, I knew I'd be in the Ohio River doing the backstroke with piranhas snapping at me."

> *Pete Gillen, on his coaching days at Xavier*

"If you want to know the turning point, it was our layup drill."

> *Darrell Hedric, Miami of Ohio coach, after losing to Purdue by 20*

"Things got so bad that I had to play the student manager for a while. Things got really bad when she started to complain to the press that she wasn't getting enough playing time."

> *Linda Hill-McDonald, Minnesota women's basketball coach, on a 6–22 season*

"The game's over, the season's over, and it's like death—you can't change it. You can't go out and say, 'Add up the score again.'"

> *Red Holzman, on a disappointing Knicks season*

"This game was an excellent argument for the NBA having a rule like boxing that allows you to throw in the towel and go home."

> *Dan Issel, after Nuggets lost to*
> *Phoenix by 30*

"Basically, what we did is follow them around, watch what they did, and foul them."

> *Rees Johnson, South Illinois coach,*
> *on losing to De Paul by 25*

"I am the worst coach of the worst division I basketball team in the country."

> *Frank Kerns, Georgia Southern*
> *basketball coach, after losing to*
> *Cornell*

"Basically, I wanted this to be a swan song, but it turned into a swan dive."

> *Jerry Reynolds, on losing his last*
> *game as Kings coach before moving*
> *to the front office*

"Sometimes you're the bug, sometimes you're the windshield. I'll leave it to you to decide which we were."

> *Kevin Smith, high school basketball coach, after his team lost by 27 points*

"I slept like a baby—I woke up and cried every two hours."

> *Fred Taylor, after losing a heartbreaking game*

"I've taken this team as far as I can."

> *Lynn Wheeler, on resigning after the Iowa State women's basketball team suffered their 14th straight loss*

"You could have locked us in a phone booth with Raquel Welch and we wouldn't have gotten our hands on anything."

> *Bob White, coach of Wisconsin–Oshkosh, on his team's defense in a 25-point loss to Navy*

"We can't win at home. We can't win on the road. As general manager, I just can't figure out where else to play."

> *Pat Williams, on the Magic's 1992 woes*

LOVE AND MARRIAGE

"I think I've got to make a strong commitment to my girlfriends and my family. Well, don't write down my girlfriends."

> *Charles Barkley, on his 1989 resolutions*

"I don't think American girls like to houseclean. . . . They talk too much."

> *Manute Bol, on marrying someone from his home country of the Sudan*

"There was a main squeeze and an older girl . . . sort of the Barbara Walters of the situation. I go to her when I need advice. We as men sometimes need someone we can talk to when women confuse us. It keeps us from jumping off buildings."

> *Elmore Spencer*

"It doesn't bother me. I was also my wife's second choice, and we've been married 25 years."

Billy Tubbs, on being second choice for the Oklahoma coaching job

MADONNA

"There would be a lot of girlfriends saying, 'No way you're going to that team.'"

Horace Grant, on Madonna wanting to own a team

"Roasting Doug Moe is like ripping the clothes off Madonna—she helps you too much."

Dick Schaap, at a roast for Moe

MAGIC

"We were so bad last year, the cheerleaders stayed home and phoned in their cheers."

Pat Williams, on the pre-Shaquille Orlando Magic

"He's the only player who can take only three shots and still dominate a game."

Julius Erving, on Magic Johnson

"He has eyes in his ears."

Chick Hearn

"They got Magic and we got tragic."

Jerry Reynolds, after Magic Johnson led the Lakers to an easy victory over the Kings

"Magic is like a politician's promise—all over the place."

Mychal Thompson

MOSES MALONE

"A dispersal draft."

> *Major Jones, asked what the Houston*
> *Rockets would be without Moses*
> *Malone*

"Moses is the Ninth Wonder of the World. Wilt Chamberlain was the Eighth."

> *George Karl*

DANNY MANNING

"He wants to go to money, but he doesn't want to be the go-to guy."

> *Dave Twardzik, on Danny Manning*

KEVIN McHALE

"I go to the mailbox, blindfolded, masked, incognito, on my knees. People say, 'Who's that four-foot-three-inch guy picking up a check?'"

Kevin McHale, on trying to be anonymous in the waning days of his career

MEDIA WATCH

"You just have to realize you can't trust the media. They're evil. I've been around it for a long time, and the media is definitely evil."

Charles Barkley

"The more attention he gets, the less I have to deal with the nitwits in the media."

Charles Barkley, on the media attention being received by Shaquille O'Neal

"It depends on what a guy is in the mood for and what you guys [writers] have been drinking."

Charles Barkley, on MVP voting

"I never realized you could get so many ugly guys together at the same time."

Charles Barkley, on being interviewed by 50 people during the All-Star Game

"I didn't even know they had this room."

Jeff Flynn, University of Cincinnati backup, answering questions in the interview room after a good game

"He and I got along just fine."

Judd Heathcote, comparing his old press conferences at Montana to those at Michigan State

"All of us learn to write by the second grade, then most of us go on to other things."

Bobby Knight, on reporters

"Dealing with the press. After the demands of the game, my mind needs a rest."

> *Bobby Knight, asked to name the*
> *part of coaching he likes best*

"I'd like to be the referee in the game that Packer and Vitale were coaching, that's my fantasy. Then I'd write the story and talk about how dumb they are as coaches."

> *Abe Lemons*

"I'm so bad that I'm good. I don't know any words that a shoeshine boy wouldn't understand."

> *Al McGuire, on his announcing*

"That's why CBS pays me . . . I hope."

> *Al McGuire, on making a good point*
> *during a game*

"I don't read the stories about myself. I just look at the pictures."

> *Shaquille O'Neal, on how he handles*
> *all the media attention*

"Jim Nantz said he never thought he'd see the day where Packer had a 65 and Nicklaus had an 81."

Billy Packer, after The Sporting News *named him the 65th-most-powerful man in sports and Nicklaus the 81st*

"Do you know what the best years of a sportswriter's life are? Third grade."

George Raveling

"I wasn't doing anything on weekends anyway."

Bill Russell, on being asked to be a commentator on NBA games

"Hubie was to network basketball ratings what the *Titanic* was to the winter cruise business."

Pat Williams, on Hubie Brown as an announcer

"Every night when you lay your head on the pillow you say, 'I'm one of 300 NBA players.' Of course, 50 of us stink really bad."
Scott Hastings

"I think the world is run by C students."
Al McGuire

"Some people say I do and some people say I don't."
Chuck Nevitt, asked by someone if he plays professional basketball

"I never knew the word 'parity.' Ten years ago, you never heard a word like that. Now everybody is talking about it. It's like cholesterol."
Kelvin Sampson, Washington State coach

MIAMI VICE

"When I approached the checkout counter of a Miami store, the clerk said, 'Cash, check, or stickup?'"

> *Pat Williams*

"Crime is down in Miami. They are out of victims."

> *Pat Williams*

DOUG MOE

"It's been consistent. When things aren't looking good, you can look at Doug and feel good about yourself."

> *Larry Brown, on his friendship with Moe*

"Mokeski looked to me like he has improved. But that's like saying Phyllis Diller is getting prettier."
Dick Vitale

MONEY MAKES THE WORLD GO 'ROUND

"I'll borrow it from my players."
> *Barry Ackerley, Supersonics owner, asked where he would get $50 million to build an arena*

"I really don't like talking about money. All I can say is that the Good Lord must have wanted me to have it."
> *Larry Bird*

"I'm getting $300,000, but over 150 years."
> *Denny Crum, on the contract he signed*

"I'm independently wealthy. I have enough money to last me the rest of my life—provided I die tomorrow."

Bill Fitch

"When I coached in college, I had one thing in common with my athletic directors—money. They wanted to save it and I wanted to spend it."

Bill Fitch

"It has a lot of doughnuts at the end."

Darrell Griffith, on his contract

"Every time I see my mother I say, 'Why didn't you wait?'"

Hot Rod Hundley, on being a first-round draft choice in 1957 and signing for $10,000

"When we started, we used to make very little money and have a lot of fun. Now we make a lot of money and have no fun at all. I like it better this way."

Abe Lemons

"They'll get a lot more hustle out of me than if I were making $270,000."

> *Vernon Maxwell, on signing a $1.6 million contract*

"I don't think basketball is the answer to all problems. If a guy comes into the league with a ton of problems, and they pay him a million dollars, then he's a millionaire with a ton of problems."

> *Kevin McHale*

"He was just lifting his suitcase. It must have had his contract in it."

> *Dick Motta, on Danny Ainge injuring his back before a game*

"When you break it down over the long haul, it's not that much."

> *Charles Tucker, Glenn Robinson's agent, on the $100 million contract that Robinson was seeking*

"I guess I'll just have to get my scoring average down."

> *Spud Webb, on Jon Koncak's six-year, $13.2 million contract*

MORGANNA

"When I saw her coming, I called for the police. I thought someone had stolen the ball bag."
Frank Layden

"We laughed, we loved, and now she's a part of me."
Chuck Nevitt, after a kiss from Morganna

"When I saw her coming at me, I thought it was a Mack truck. I figured I had two options: either get hit or get out of the way. I decided to get hit."
Kelly Tripucka

MOVIE TIME

"We call him Chevy Chase. He's over here on a European Vacation."
Charles Barkley, on John Stockton, who injured himself before the 1992 Olympics in Barcelona

"Last year I got booed for not liking *City Slickers*. You have to be tough to give a bad review to a western in Dallas."

> *Ron "Popeye" Jones, on reviewing*
> *movies before Mavericks games and*
> *being criticized for giving too many*
> *positive reviews*

MUSCLE BEACH

"You can't get much stronger than an onion, and he's stronger than six rows of 'em."

> *Benny Dees, on 6'7", 250-pound*
> *Reginald Slater*

"It's a three-second violation just to drive around him."

> *Chick Hearn on the physique of*
> *Lonnie Shelton*

"He looks like he worked on the Nautilus all summer. Either that, or he carried the machine in every day."

> *John Killelea, Bucks assistant coach,*
> *on Dave Corzine*

"I told the guys that they have been looking like so many maître d's when what I wanted was bouncers. A maître d' shows you to a table. A bouncer busts you over the head with it."

> *Frank Layden, on the passive play of the Jazz*

"He's so strong that he could be the first guy in college basketball to pop a ball."

> *Stan Morrison, USC coach, on 6′9″, 240-pound Clayton Oliver*

"That guy has muscles in places most people don't have places."

> *Bucky Waters, on Tom Hammonds*

NAME GAME

"Now that I'm in Detroit, I'd like to change my name from M. L. Carr to Abdul Automobile."

> *M. L. Carr*

"We've got two kids named Art coming in next year. You can have them both to work with."

> *Pete Carril, on asking assistant coach*
> *Armond Hill to devote less time to*
> *his love of art and more to basketball*

"You can soon start calling me World B. Free Agent."

> *World B. Free, on being a free agent*

"I think I'll name my firstborn son Extermin. That way he'll be Extermin Nater."

> *Swen Nater*

"The latest is Procastin Nater."

> *Swen Nater, on possible names for*
> *his son*

NETS

"Play some Picasso."

> *Chris Morris, asking assistant Nets*
> *coach Rick Carlisle for a special*
> *request while Carlisle was playing*
> *the piano*

"I was driving on the highway in New Jersey and saw a sign. It said, 'Interstate 95, Nets 91.'"
                    John Salley

NEW YORK, NEW YORK

"I own a gun."
                    Charles Barkley, on why he loves New York

"I come from New York, where if you fall down, someone will pick you up by the wallet."
                    Al McGuire

"Complaining about the altitude is like us complaining about the pollution in New York."
                    Doug Moe, after some Knicks players blamed a loss in Denver on the high altitude

"I asked a guy what time it was, and he said to me, 'What do I look like, a clock?' That's when I knew I was home."
                    Jim Valvano, on coming back to New York

"He used to be able to jump over a quarter pounder. He's done some work on his legs. Now he can jump over a Big Mac."

> *Charles Barkley, on why he calls*
> *teammate Mark McNamara Big Mac*

"I thought he had tremendous publicity possibilities. . . . After a few workouts, the other players gave him a nickname of their own. It was 'Not too.'"

> *Shelby Metcalf, on recruiting a*
> *player named Sharp*

NORTH CAROLINA

"This is a great school. Look at all the alumni who are in the NBA."

> *Brian Reese, on the University of*
> *North Carolina*

NORTH CAROLINA STATE

"What do you say to an N.C. State athlete in a three-piece suit? . . . Will the defendant please stand?"

Anonymous

"I made a ridiculous statement when I first went to North Carolina State. I said I know basketball down there was like life or death. I was very wrong. It's more important."

Jim Valvano

"They had a big scandal at his school—three players were found in the library."

Pat Williams, on Jim Valvano and North Carolina State

ON THE ROAD AGAIN

"After all the traveling I have done, I demand to be called an international disgrace."

John Chaney, on Howard Cosell calling him a national disgrace

"Any player who says bus or plane has to run suicide sprints."

> *Bob Hallberg, Chicago State coach, on spending 18 of 22 days on the road*

"Good. Bad. OK. Terrible. OK. Bad. And Good."

> *Phil Jackson, assessing a seven-game Bulls road trip*

"Start a rumor that you're looking for a road game."

> *Abe Lemons, on the best way to draw a crowd at a basketball convention*

"The trip must have been planned by the Marquis de Sade Travel Agency."

> *Jack Marin, on five road games in seven days*

ORLANDO

"If it weren't for the bowling alleys in this town, there would be no culture at all."

> *Pat Williams*

"I like to take transfers especially from the PAC 10, because the new cars already have been paid for."
Jerry Tarkanian

PAIN IN THE . . .

"All it means is that people will say I don't have the biggest butt in the league anymore."
Charles Barkley, on what it means having Rick Mahorn as a teammate

"If we named an all-rear team, this guy would be the captain."
Al McGuire, on Missouri player Michael Walker

"He's got such a low center of gravity. And by low center of gravity, I mean he's got a big butt. He's definitely got a butt that would win any big-butt contest he enters."
Mychal Thompson, on Charles Barkley

PLAYGROUND

"The rule was 'No autopsy, no foul.'"
> *Stewart Granger, on tough childhood*
> *pickup games in which he was*
> *involved*

"Playgrounds are the best place to learn the game,
because if you lose you sit down."
> *Gary Williams*

PLAYOFF TIME

"Getting close counts only in horseshoes, hand
grenades, and drive-in movies."
> *Bill Fitch, on his team coming close*
> *to making the playoffs*

"They go on and on. It's like a guy telling a bad
joke for 15 minutes."
> *Tom Heinsohn, on the playoffs*

"If you don't go to the prom, you don't get to dance with the queen."

> *Frank Layden, on the Jazz making the playoffs*

"I don't care if we get it in Alaska."

> *Moses Malone, asked if he wanted to win the championship in Philadelphia or Los Angeles*

"It's not like backgammon or cribbage, where if you beat someone bad enough you get two wins."

> *Cedric Maxwell, on the Celtics winning the first game of a playoff series by a huge amount*

"It's not as challenging now that they expanded the playoffs. All you have to do is make a team in the fall, still be breathing in the spring, and you're in."

> *Billy Paultz, on participating in post-season play 13 years in a row*

"Score seven more points."

> *Doc Rivers, asked to name the Knicks' goal for the 1994–95 season after the team lost Game 7 of the 1993–94 finals by six points*

"They're not my type. I like to be around low-class people like reporters."

Charles Barkley, on not attending Clinton's inauguration

"My family got all over me because they said Bush is only for the rich people. Then I reminded them, 'Hey, I'm rich.'"

Charles Barkley, on voting for George Bush for President

"If I ever go to Russia and meet with Gorbachev, the news stories will start with, 'Bill Bradley, former New York Knick.'"

Bill Bradley

"Line them up and let them shoot jump shots from the key."

Bill Bradley, on how the Democrats should choose a presidential candidate

"If the Republicans can rebound from Watergate, I'm sure Tulane can rebound from that."

> *Perry Clark, Tulane coach, after a point-shaving scandal at the school*

"Mr. Jennings needed work. The university needed his son. It was a worthy cause."

> *Harry Davis, assistant to Kentucky governor Happy Chandler, on hiring the father of Kentucky center Ned Jennings to work on a highway crew*

"I suppose if I was offered enough money I'd try the pros. Everybody has his price. For enough money, I'd become a Communist. Well, maybe not a Communist. A Democrat, anyway."

> *Abe Lemons, asked if he ever considered coaching in the NBA*

"Most of the brothers don't make the kind of scratch I do."

> *Cedric Maxwell, on why he voted for the conservative Jesse Helms to represent North Carolina in the Senate*

"It was the first time in my life I was happy to see zero after my name."

> *Tom McMillen, former NBA player and congressman, on having no bounced checks in the congressional check-writing scandal*

"He just up and told me he wanted to be President. . . . He certainly shows promise at being a politician, switching positions whenever it becomes advantageous."

> *Stan Morrison, on star recruit Lamar Flatl, who left USC for Harvard*

"You mean there aren't enough people mad at me already?"

> *President Ronald Reagan, on being presented with a referee's jacket during a visit by the basketball commissioner*

POLLS

"I don't like anybody telling me I ain't good."
> *Lefty Driesell, on why he likes his team ranked high early in the season*

"The only Pole I pay attention to is my mother."

*Mike Krzyzewski, on Duke going
down in the polls*

"You mean in the state?"

*Abe Lemons, on being asked if the
University of Texas should be ranked
in the Top 20*

"First because we deserve it, second because I'm on
the rating committee."

*Herb Magee, Philadelphia Textile
coach, on his team ranking in the
Top 10 of small schools*

"I'd rather eat macaroni."

*Rollie Massimino, on the significance
of Villanova being first in the Big
East in mid-January*

"If we're number 17 in the nation, it's a sick
nation."

*Wimp Sanderson, on a preseason poll
that ranked Alabama 17th*

"I think someone slipped a virus into that computer."

> *John Sneed, Cal State–Fullerton*
> *coach, on being ranked 9th in* USA
> Today's *computer rankings*

"*Playboy* picked us eighth [in Big 8]. I didn't see it. I didn't get past the centerfold."

> *Billy Tubbs, on Oklahoma*

PRACTICE

"One day of practice is like one day of clean living. It doesn't do you any good."

> *Abe Lemons*

"I just wanted to be ready for a quick getaway."

> *Abe Lemons, on why he was wearing*
> *a coat during practice*

"When you are not practicing, remember someone is practicing, and when you meet him, he will win."

> *Ed Macauley*

"I'm not going to allow him to pick up our baby until it's at least five years old."

Wife of Ed Nealy, after he dropped several passes in a game

"I'm a little nervous. My sister is expecting a baby, and I'm wondering if I'm going to be an aunt or an uncle."

Chuck Nevitt

"I have at least one advantage over men coaches. If my son grew up to be a basketball player, my feelings won't be hurt if he doesn't want to play for me."

Pat Head Summitt, University of Tennessee women's basketball coach, on being pregnant with a boy

PRESSURE

"It's when you look at a cheerleader and don't notice her body."

Al McGuire, on pressure games

"I don't know if I was nervous, but I was scared to death."

Tom Santel, Austin Peay player, asked if he was nervous before his opening game

PRO LIFE

"At least when I called a time-out in college, I knew I was the best-paid guy in the huddle."

Ed Badger, assistant coach of the Hornets, on the difference between the NBA and college

"I want a dollar more than the highest-paid star, and I want the owner to stay away. How is that going to happen?"

Al McGuire, on why he never coached in the pros

"We get nice per diem checks and we stay in nice hotels and we don't have to carry our luggage."

Jerry Tarkanian, on life in the NBA as opposed to college

RAIN DELAY

"I'm an experienced guy. I've been around a long time and seen a lot of water delays. There is a real knack in how you handle them."

Doug Moe, on a water leak holding up a game eventually won by the Nuggets

JACK RAMSAY

"Jack Ramsay was the kind of basketball coach who, anytime we were 8 points behind with four seconds left to play, he'd get down on his knee and figure out a 9-point play."

Bill Walton

REACH OUT
AND TOUCH SOMEONE

"I think the whole game hinged on one call—the one I made last April scheduling the game."

Peter Gavett, women's basketball coach at Maine, after losing to Virginia 115–53

"Look for a rate hike."

Bill Russell, on being asked how much money he got for a telephone commercial

"We're playing the Bell Telephone defense. You know, reach out and touch someone."

Bob Wenzel, former Jacksonville coach, on his team averaging 25 fouls a game

REBOUNDS

"I wish we could get Robey back here. Then I could get my offensive rebounding average back up."

Larry Bird, on former teammate Rick Robey

"When I saw two players flying over the rim, I thought we would be a great rebounding team. Then someone told me it was an earthquake."

Jim Brovelli, University of San Francisco basketball coach

"You figure you've got to get one rebound or you'd only have as many as Elvis or any other dead guy."

Scott Hastings, on players who score no points, have no fouls, and get no rebounds during a game

"I never thought I'd lead the NBA in rebounding, but I got a lot of help from my teammates—they did a lot of missing."

Moses Malone

"My nine-year-old daughter could run around out there for 27 minutes, and two rebounds would hit her on the head."

Gary Williams, during his coaching days at American University, on his top rebounder getting one rebound in 27 minutes

RECRUITMENT

"This ought to help our recruiting. Now the kids will know they can play if they sign with us."

Ed Badger, former University of Cincinnati coach, on losing a televised game by 40 points

"I'd suggest he go back to North Dakota and give the Sioux their land back, because we're just renting it."

> *Dale Brown, on Louisiana legislator Mike Thompson being against LSU's recruitment of Arvidas Sabonis from the USSR*

"Some of my best recruiting has been done over a turkey and pastrami club."

> *Lou Carnesecca*

"I can't even get kids to visit from California. They all think I'm Andy Griffith."

> *Benny Dees, Wyoming coach, on the difficulties he has in recruiting*

"I spent 45 minutes trying to recruit the thing. I thought he could be an inside force for us."

> *Tommy Joe Eagles, former Auburn coach, on seeing a moose during the Great Alaska Shootout*

"Of the guys we want, there aren't too many who can spell calculus, let alone take it."

> *Paul Evans, on the difficulty he had recruiting at Navy*

"It was getting so bad that whenever the phone rang, I was afraid to answer. I told my parents if it was a man to tell him I wasn't home, and if it was a girl that I would be right there."

Todd Krueger, highly recruited high school player

"Just once I'd like to see a picture of one of those guys with the caption 'He's a dog. Ate $8,000 worth of groceries in four years and can't play worth a lick.'"

Abe Lemons, on player profiles in press brochures

"They always tell you how tall the kid is going to be when he grows up. The one mother wrote that her son was 6 feet but she knew he would be taller because he had an uncle 6'8". I told her we would just recruit the uncle."

Abe Lemons, on parents of recruits

"All you have to do is limit each coach to $10,000 a year and tell him he can keep whatever he doesn't spend."

Abe Lemons, on the best way to reduce recruiting costs

"I just can't recruit where there's grass around. You gotta have a concrete lawn before I feel comfortable enough to go in and talk to your parents."

Al McGuire

"A summer camp is like castor oil—you may not like it, but you've got to take it."

George Raveling, on summer camps that evaluate top high-school players

"It takes two visits before somebody won't laugh at our name."

Charles Spoonhour, former coach at Southwest Missouri State, on the difficulty in recruiting there

"I'll watch the kids play, have a big steak with my friends, stay in a nice hotel, sign a lot of autographs, then go back to Vegas and tell my alumni how tough recruiting is."

Jerry Tarkanian

"We sat down and had a personal discussion about it. I gave him a letter of intent and told him to get the baby's footprint."

John Thompson, on attempting to recruit Patrick Ewing's one-year-old son

"I took him to our school cafeteria and he ordered a mint julep."

Jim Valvano, explaining how he knew recruit Rodney McRae would end up at Louisville instead of North Carolina State

"I used to go up to kids and say, 'Hi, Jim Valvano, Iona College.' And the kid would say, 'Wow, you must be the youngest dude in the country who owns a college.'"

Jim Valvano

"You know how some years you recruit guards, and some years big men. This year I recruited feet."

Jim Valvano, on four incoming players having size 15 feet or larger

"We don't need refs, but I guess white guys need something to do. All the players are black."
Charles Barkley

"The trouble with officials is they just don't care who wins."
Tommy Canterbury, former
Centenary coach

"The only thing tougher than being a basketball referee is being happily married."
Skip Caray

"When we came out on the floor and I saw Looie and the three refs deciding where they were gonna eat right after the game."
Tom Green, Farleigh Dickinson
coach, asked when he knew he was
in for a long night against St. John's,
coached by Lou Carnesecca

"It just gives you one more to yell at."
Dale Clayton, assistant coach at
Vanderbilt, on having three referees

"Most of them are like me. They can't see anymore."

> *Lefty Driesell, on referees*

"I liked the officials. They couldn't understand a word I was saying."

> *Lefty Driesell, on playing in a tournament in Mexico City*

"If you put the brains of three officials in a hummingbird, it would still fly backwards."
> *Bill Fitch*

"Our guys are handling the rush-hour traffic and the college guys can't even handle the Sunday drivers."

> *Bill Fitch, on the difference in officiating between college and the pros*

"We'll play them anywhere we can get three good referees who aren't Catholic."

> *Gene Keady, Purdue coach, on playing against Notre Dame*

"Who are you calling a fool? You paid to watch this game."

> *Frank Layden, addressing a fan who called a referee a fool during an awful Jazz performance*

"You can say something to popes, kings, presidents, but you can't talk to officials. In the next war, they ought to give everybody a whistle."

> *Abe Lemons*

"I don't know who they'll be for tomorrow night. But give them a bottle of Geritol and they'll be ready to go again."

> *Abe Lemons, on a badly officiated game*

"I loved it. I could yell at the refs, and they couldn't do anything to me."

> *Dick Motta, on being a TV commentator*

"Our team meshed well with the officials. We shot 32 percent and the officials got about that many calls right."

> *Lynn Nance, former Iowa State coach*

"Rookie call, brother. I'm going to be a vet next year and I'm going to get all the calls. I'm going to be going to the line all the time—just like Karl Malone, just like Jordan."

> *Shaquille O'Neal, after he was called for traveling in a game during his rookie year*

"If the Warren Commission were still active, I'd send them a tape to determine whether one official acted alone or if there was a conspiracy."

> *George Raveling, on sending a videotape of a game to PAC 10 officials to protest the officiating of a game*

"Incompetence should not be confined to one sex."
> *Bill Russell, on female referees*

"Officiating is the only occupation in the world where the highest accolade is silence."
> *Earl Strom*

"Once I was jumping up and down after a bad call. He gave me a technical for bad dancing."
> *Wes Unseld, on Hall of Fame referee Earl Strom*

REFORMS

"No referees. Players should call their own fouls, just like on the playground. Some guys already have that worked out."

> *Jerry Reynolds, asked for his ideas*
> *for improving basketball*

"All Italian coaches should be given lifetime contracts."

> *Jim Valvano, on changes he would*
> *like to see in college basketball*

RELIGION

"He's so devout that if you drive by a church, he'll ask you to turn the radio down."

> *Dale Brown, on Chris Jackson*

"If you're going to the Final Four, you have to recruit athletes, not Christians."

> *Lake Kelly, Oral Roberts coach, on*
> *the difficulties of recruiting at Oral*
> *Roberts*

"I had a bad dream the other day. God sneezed and I didn't know what to say to him."

Frank Layden

"I don't think Oral would want me. I smoke, and I ain't going to give up cigars just to coach."

Abe Lemons, on rumors of his being offered the coaching job at Oral Roberts

"If the Eleventh Commandment was 'Thou shalt not covet thy neighbor's players,' I'd be on the way to hell, big time."

Rick Majerus, Utah coach, on stealing players from Brigham Young University

"What makes you think God loves wimps?"

David Robinson, asked if being born again makes him a less aggressive player

"I'm not Catholic."

John Salley, asked how he could convert the former house of the Detroit archbishop into a bachelor pad

"I don't know. What's his number?"

> *Billy Tubbs, asked if God was on his opponents' side after a tough loss*

"The good father did a great job for us. When we fell 65 points behind, he started administering last rites."

> *Jim Valvano, on coaching at Bucknell and having a priest on the bench during a tough loss*

RETIREMENT

"I didn't miss the smell of the gym, the bounce of the ball, or the kids. I just ran out of money."

> *Bob Boyd, on why he came out of retirement to coach Mississippi State*

"Most people didn't notice that at his retirement press conference, Michael's microphone went dead for a few minutes. What he was saying during that time was that it made no sense to keep playing now that he no longer had Scott Hastings to compete against. There was just no challenge for him any longer."

> *Scott Hastings, on retiring the same time as Jordan*

"When I saw my team play."

> *Abe Lemons, asked when he knew it was time to retire*

"When you look in our media guide and see in a guy's profile that his favorite music is Heavy D, well . . . That's a sign I lost it. Actually, I did know one person that was mentioned. I got one player going to be a doctor. He said Mozart."

> *Abe Lemons, on knowing when it was time to retire*

"The trouble with retirement is that you never get a day off."

> *Abe Lemons*

"I would like to retire, but I can't afford it. So I have to keep coaching, because I can't do anything else."

> *Doug Moe*

"Sports is the only profession I know that when you retire, you have to go to work."

> *Earl Monroe*

THE RETURN OF MR. JORDAN

"His hair."

> *Ron Harper, asked if Michael Jordan had lost anything upon returning from his 20-month hiatus from basketball*

"With Michael Jordan, Yakima (a CBA team) could be an NBA championship contender. The man is that good."

> *Kenny Smith, on the impact to the Bulls of Jordan's return*

"We're not eating, we're not sleeping. We're like Gandhi."

> *Pete Gillen, former Xavier coach, on preparing for archrival Cincinnati*

"We haven't won at Dayton since before the Russian Revolution. Rasputin was in junior high school."

> *Pete Gillen, on Xavier playing at Dayton*

"They're no different than us. They put on their bras just like we do."

> *Lynn Norenberg, guard at William and Mary, on not being intimidated by rival Old Dominion*

"It's ugly. I took it down to Miami Beach and it's so ugly the tide refused to come in."

> *Pat Williams, on the trophy Orlando received for winning the in-state rivalry with the Miami Heat*

"Sort of like having cheese steak on pita bread."
Alexander Wolff, Sports Illustrated writer, on the curtailing of Philadelphia's Big Four series, featuring Villanova, St. Joseph's, LaSalle, and Temple

STANLEY ROBERTS

"He doesn't get angry. If you call him fat, he turns the other chin."
Pat Williams

"Now he combines them both by eating out of his satellite dish."
Pat Williams, on Roberts combining his two favorite things, eating and watching television

"He thinks a balanced meal is a Big Mac in each hand."
Pat Williams

"Stanley Roberts's Florida license says, 'Photo continued on other side.'"

Pat Williams

"We told Stanley to go on a water diet, and Lake Superior disappeared."

Pat Williams

"Stanley's chosen his burial site—Montana."

Pat Williams

"He could be the 1991 poster boy for jelly doughnuts."

Pat Williams

"You know the old saying, 'No man is an island.' Stanley comes close."

Pat Williams

"We got him eating the seven basic food groups, and now there are only three left."

Pat Williams

"I can't use the fat jokes anymore. Stanley has turned over a new chin."

> *Pat Williams, on Roberts's efforts to lose weight*

"McDonald's and Wendy's are suing Stanley for nonsupport."

> *Pat Williams, on Roberts's continuing efforts to lose weight*

RICK ROBEY

"I pay Robey more than anyone to come to my summer basketball camp. The kids can watch him play and see for themselves what not to do."

> *Larry Bird*

ROOKIES

"I tried to match it."

> *Jim Valvano, on Chris Washburn turning pro and making a million dollars a year*

"How can you haze rookies when they all make more money than you do?"
Kiki Vandeweghe

BILL RUSSELL

"Young man, you have the question backwards."
Bill Russell, after a reporter asked him how he would have fared against Kareem Abdul-Jabbar

SCHEDULE

"We just finished playing our 'God and Country' schedule and might have a lot of folks mad at us."
Paul Hansen, former Oklahoma State coach, on beating both Oral Roberts and Air Force

"When I give a lecture, I look for the guy who's taking notes. That's who I want to schedule next year."
Abe Lemons

"Coaches who shoot par in the summer are the guys I want on my schedule in the winter."

Abe Lemons

"There are a lot of guys who played tough schedules who are working at Kmart."

George Raveling, on playing a lot of home games when he coached at Iowa

"We don't have a fight song. We have a surrender song."

Glenn Wilkes, Stetson coach, on a schedule that featured Duke, Florida State, and Wake Forest

SCHOOL DAYS

"I can safely say I was in the top 10 percent. As a matter of fact, I've gone up to number one, because five or six years ago the school burned and all the records went with it."

Lou Henson, on his high school in Oklahoma, which had 13 students

"We had a lot of nicknames—Scarface, Blackie, Toothless. And those were just the cheerleaders."

Frank Layden, on his high school days in Brooklyn

"If you went to my school with two ears, it was obvious you were a transfer student."

George Raveling, on growing up in a tough area

SCORING

"How are the Dallas Mavericks like a man with four 20 dollar bills? Neither one of them can break a hundred."

Anonymous, on an anemic offensive Mavericks team

"This year we plan to run and shoot. Next year, we hope to run and score."

Billy Tubbs

"This team gives me the ball in such fantastic position that you could be a blind man with one leg and still score."

Buck Williams, on his high field-goal percentage

SCOUTING REPORT

"I hate to see the pro scouts sitting so close to the floor. It tends to give the players peripheral vision."
Al McGuire

"Last year he thought a scouting report consisted of whether we were red or white that night."

Bob Weiss, on the improved preparation and play of Kevin Willis

76ERS

"I know there is something I'm going to miss about Philadelphia, but I don't know what it is yet."

John Block, after being traded from the 76ers

"Hey, I was with Philadelphia."

> *Jeff Hornacek, explaining his positive*
> *outlook after being traded to Utah*
> *with his wife expecting a child in*
> *May, when the playoffs would be in*
> *full swing*

SHAQ ATTACK

"Legally? Maybe triple-team him with big bodies."

> *Elgin Baylor, asked what is the best*
> *way to defend against Shaquille*
> *O'Neal*

"It's like standing next to a house. It's like trying to get around a Cadillac. It's like an upside-down Christmas tree. Coach Fitch said if I get my sixth foul I could bite him."

> *Matt Fish, on guarding Shaq*

"You throw up an air ball and then Shaq goes up 15 feet to catch it and dunk it, and everyone says, 'Wow, what a pass.'"

> *Anfernee Hardaway*

"If he got any meaner, there wouldn't be a league."
Rick Mahorn, asked if Shaq needed
to get meaner to succeed in the NBA

"I'm only 13."
Shaquille O'Neal, after Dale Brown
first met him at a basketball clinic on
a military base in West Germany and
asked him how much time he had
left in the service

"Maybe it's because I smile. Mourning doesn't smile that much, bro. I have nice teeth, and I'm very handsome."
Shaquille O'Neal, on why he is more
popular than Alonzo Mourning

"He has a hard body. It was like colliding with a 10-story building."
Robert Parish, on Shaq

"That's like looking at Barbra Streisand and saying she's got a crooked nose."
Lee Rose, NBA assistant coach, on
Shaq's lack of a jump shot

"Pray for a hurricane."

> *Gary St. Jean, on the best way to*
> *stop a Shaq Attack*

"I told my team not to worry about Shaquille
O'Neal. He puts his pants on the same way we do,
only four feet higher."

> *Billy Tubbs, on preparing for a game*
> *against LSU*

"Shaquille's house is in such a great neighborhood
the bird feeders have salad bars."

> *Pat Williams*

SHOOT 'EM UP

"He has the shooting range. What he doesn't have
is the making range."

> *Pete Carril, on moving Steve*
> *Goodrich from center to forward*

"Sometimes we have to remind Demetrius that you don't get extra points for degrees of difficulty."

Roy Chipman, former Pittsburgh coach, on the shot selection of Demetrius Gore

"Some guy yelled, 'Hey, Malone, pass the ball for a change and stop shooting so much!' I went 5-for-5 after that. What if I listened to that guy?"

Jeff Malone

"I like to take all the shots in tough situations. As a matter of fact, I like taking all the shots."

Mike Mitchell

"When I step into the building, you've got to get me the ball. When I step off the bus, I'm open."

Chuck Person

"I wouldn't want my guys to play you guys [the media] in HORSE right now."

Eddie Sutton, on the poor shooting of his Oklahoma State team

"All I have to do is be in the arena."

Trent Tucker, on his shooting range

"They have to put plugs in the drain when he takes a shower."

> *Chick Hearn, on the skinny Michael Cooper*

"He'll be a professional star for at least 30 years—2 as a center in the NBA and 28 as the left-field foul pole in Wrigley Field."

> *Tony Kornheiser,* Washington Post *columnist, on Shawn Bradley*

"If he ever gets a hangin' offense, they could never hang 'em up. His rear end isn't big enough to snap the rope."

> *Sonny Smith, on 6'11", 195-pound Matt Geiger*

"He is so skinny, he can stand on a clothesline in a rainstorm."

> *Sonny Smith, on Chris Morris*

SLEEP

"Some people live to eat. I live to sleep."

> *Sam Perkins, on the great joy of*
> *his life*

"Not true. My wide-screen TV is in my bedroom, and I am a bed potato."

> *Dwayne Schintzius, denying that he*
> *is a couch potato*

"On videotapes of Big East games they have a disclaimer that says, 'Caution: May Cause Drowsiness.'"

> *Billy Tubbs, on the defensive nature*
> *of the Big East teams*

SMILE AND THE WORLD SMILES WITH YOU

"I have three versions—the million-dollar smile, the $2 million, and the $3 million."

> *Shaquille O'Neal, on his smile*

DEAN SMITH

"I told Dick Motta [Kings coach] to practice the four-corner offense when he got to Carolina in honor of Dean Smith."

> *Jerry Reynolds, on the Kings scoring*
> *59 points in a loss to Charlotte*

SOCCER

"The biggest challenge I faced as a coach was when I coached the Lafayette soccer team, when I had never played soccer."

> *Gary Williams, asked if a difficult*
> *year at Maryland was his biggest*
> *challenge as a coach*

SPEED

"The kid is slower than erosion."

> *Gordon Chiesa, former Manhattan*
> *coach, on Tim Cain*

"I knew it was time to retire when I was driving down the lane and I got called for a three-second violation."

> *Johnny Kerr*

"He's as quick as the last Mass at a summer resort."

> *Al McGuire, on former player Dean Meminger*

SPORTS SECTION

"Don't bother. Somebody already swiped the sports section."

> *Mark Landsberger, after throwing down the* Wall Street Journal *and seeing a teammate pick it up*

STADIUMS

"What I don't understand is how come there are no gas pumps in the Arco Arena?"

> *Danny Ainge, on playing in the Arco Arena in Sacramento*

"I love it. It's a cross between Boston Garden and my garage."

> *Matt Melvin, Central (Iowa) forward, on Penn Gymnasium, home of rival William Penn*

"It was the coldest gym I ever played in. A couple of rebounds came down with frost on them."

> *Brooke Steppe, on the Pontiac Silverdome*

JOHN STOCKTON

"He has a lot of things going for him. He's Irish Catholic, he laughs at my jokes, and his dad owns a bar."

> *Frank Layden*

STRATEGY

"What strategy? If you're behind in the last two minutes, you foul. If you're ahead, you hold on to the ball. That's all there is to it."

> *Doug Moe, on critics who say college basketball has more strategy than the NBA*

"When Xavier McDaniel plays against Orlando Woolridge, it's a coach's dream—X versus O."
> *Mychal Thompson*

STREAKS

"I'm tired of breaking all of them. I'd like to get one of our own."

> *Cotton Fitzsimmons, former coach of the Suns, on ending three opponents' winning streaks in a two-week period*

SUBSTITUTIONS

"**W**ittman in for debauchery."

> *Mike Wittman, University of Miami*
> *player, telling the officials whom he*
> *was replacing when entering a game*

SUPERSTITION

"**O**ne, don't call somebody a bad name if they're
holding a loaded pistol. Two, don't call your
girlfriend Tina if her name is Vivian."

> *George Underwood, East Tennessee*
> *player, asked if he had any*
> *superstitions*

TAKES A LICKIN'

"**S**ometimes I think they think I'm a Timex watch. I
hope I can keep on ticking."

> *Kareem Abdul-Jabbar, on the physical*
> *abuse he took on a regular basis*

"Do you want a man-to-man or a zone?"

> *Tamer Shteinhaur, after being asked*
> *by South Florida teammate Radenko*
> *Dobra to guard his watch during a*
> *game*

TALK TOO MUCH

"I guess he won't be talking for a few years."

> *Charles Barkley, on Moses Malone's*
> *vow that he would remain silent until*
> *the Bullets reached the .500 mark*

"The only time I worry is when my mouth goes numb."

> *Charles Barkley, on his legs going*
> *numb during a practice*

"No comment."

> *Doug Moe, on being named to the*
> *NBA All-Interview Team*

"I'm going to be talking trash, down 80 or up 20."

> *Chuck Person*

"As long as they don't put a cast on my tongue, I'm OK."

> *Dick Vitale, on breaking his wrist*
> *while swinging a golf club*

TEAMWORK

"Those [big games] are the games you've got to play team ball to win. I get fired up for the small games. You can get your average up in a hurry and then go sit down."

> *Darryl Kennedy, Oklahoma player*

"For a bunch of guys who would rather pass kidney stones than a basketball, it was pretty amazing."

> *Bob Weiss, on the teamwork of the*
> *Hawks*

TECHNICAL FOUL

"The ref said I violated 10:10. I don't know if he meant a basketball rule or a verse and chapter of the Bible."

Jim Valvano, commenting on being assessed a technical foul

"Technical fouls are like traffic tickets. Sometimes you might deserve one and don't get it, but when you do, you don't think you deserved it."

John Wooden

TELEVISION

"With Rick on the show, they could call it the stupid human trick, or stupid pet trick because Rick is an animal."

Charles Barkley, on Rick Mahorn's appearance on The Late Show with David Letterman

"The way I figure it, with me doing TV—everybody's going to stay home and watch me. The ACC will have to get me a coaching job or attendance will go down and they'll go broke."

Lefty Driesell, on becoming an announcer of ACC games

"Chuck went from the worst shot in the East to the best shot in the West."

Tom Heinsohn, on Chuck Connors going from being a bad shooting basketball player to starring in The Rifleman

"I thought television was a fad."

Al McGuire, on not being 100 percent accurate on all his predictions

"I'm not that encouraged. I told my wife I looked like a fat little hillbilly. She said, 'That's because you are, dear.'"

Jerry Reynolds, commenting on a television appearance he made

"That's pretty good. When Fernando Martin comes back from his injury, they'll be able to have a Laugh-In with Rowan and Martin."

Mychal Thompson, after Portland signed Ron Rowan

TEMPER, TEMPER

"I just wanted to show the crowd my tailored shirt."

Ed Badger, on getting upset and slamming his coat on the floor during a game

"His range during a game is from mad to very mad."

Tom McMillan, on longtime NBA coach Hubie Brown

"I would be concerned with Charles's tolerance with people who disagree with him. He once told me that everyone is entitled to his own stupid opinion."

Pat Williams, on Charles Barkley

"Too bad he wasn't 40 today."

> *Ed Bilik, coach of Springfield, on*
> *Ivan Olivares scoring 24 points on*
> *his 24th birthday*

"It was my birthday. I was born on the 53rd of November."

> *Darryl Dawkins, on why he wears*
> *number 53*

THREE-POINTERS

"We're good at shooting threes. We're just not good at making them."

> *Sonny Smith, coach at Virginia*
> *Commonwealth Edison*

"I'm not saying the circle is too close, but at halftime my mother came out of the stands and knocked in three out of four."

> *Jim Valvano, on 19-foot three-pointers*

TIMBERWOLVES

"Come on, there'll always be tickets. We still play the Timberwolves."

> *Susan O'Malley, Bullets president, on all the sellouts the Bullets had after they acquired Chris Webber*

TIME OUT

"The last time-out was to take the sandwich order."

> *Ed Murphy, basketball coach at Mississippi, on why he took a time-out with two minutes left down by 20*

"I'm not smart enough to talk to my players that many times. After the fourth time-out in the first half, I told 'em to stay out there. I didn't have anything to say."

> *Jerry Pimm, former Utah coach*

"One of these days he'll become a sophomore."
> *Julius Smith, assistant coach at*
> *Mississippi State, on freshman Robert*
> *Woodard calling a time-out when*
> *none were left*

"I don't like all the TV time-outs. I run out of things to say to my team."
> *Jim Valvano*

"The time-outs smell a lot better."
> *Butch van Breda Kolff, longtime*
> *basketball coach, on why he enjoys*
> *coaching a female team better than*
> *his old teams*

TO BE OR NOT TO BE

"He's the only guy in history who has played both Hamlet and Portland."
> *Carnie Edison, on Paul Westhead, a*
> *Shakespearean scholar and*
> *basketball coach*

TONGUE-LASHING

"A radio guy asked me how long my tongue was."
Michael Jordan, on the dumbest
question he was ever asked

TOUGH ENOUGH

"Now I know how Mike Tyson's opponents feel. But if I'm going to get $25 million for it, I don't mind getting knocked out."
Magic Johnson, on being knocked out
in a game against the Bulls

"When the going gets tough, the tough go fishing."
Merv Lopes, Chaminade (Hawaii)
coach, on player motivation

"I imagine I would get things like letter bombs, knives, axes, maybe even some poison candy."
Maurice Lucas, NBA tough guy,
imagining his farewell tour from
the NBA

"I'm a blue-collar worker. I don't punch in. I punch out."

Maurice Lucas

"I do what it takes to win—if it kills me or if it kills you."

Rick Mahorn, on his rough play

"The neighborhood where I grew up was so tough, the Avon Lady was Sonny Liston."

George Raveling

TOURNAMENT TIME

"I turned to my wife and said: 'The phone's gonna start ringing in the morning.'"

Fred Brown, Georgetown player who mistakenly passed the ball to North Carolina's James Worthy in the final seconds of the 1983 NCAA finals, after Chris Webber called a time-out with none left in the final seconds of the 1993 finals against North Carolina

"Tell your kids to look ahead to finals—that is, final exams."

> *Bill Cosby, after learning 16th-seed Lehigh would play number-one seed Georgetown in the first round of the NCAA Tournament*

"We are the hors d'oeuvres of the NCAA Tournament."

> *Pete Gillen, on Xavier losing in the first round of the NCAA Tournament two years in a row*

"We're going to a sword fight with a toothpick."

> *Billy Lee, Campbell University coach, on facing number-one seed Duke in the first round of the NCAA Tournament*

"It's not important which dance you go to; it's just important that you go to a dance."

> *Rick Majerus, on Utah going to the NIT, not the NCAA Tournament*

"It's like getting all the dances with the girl, but when it comes time to take her home and get in the rumble seat, it's CBS that is touchin' the soft spots."

Al McGuire, NBC analyst, on CBS getting telecast rights to the NCAA Tournament

"You don't like to play teams with hyphens."
Jim Valvano, on North Carolina State narrowly winning a tournament game against Arkansas–Little Rock

"They think Pepperdine is a brand of chewing gum."

Jim Valvano, on getting his North Carolina State team psyched up to play Pepperdine in the first round of the NCAA Tournament

"I just hope that when Gene Sullivan dies and goes to heaven, he doesn't find the admitting is done by a selection committee."

Reverend E. Corbette Walsh, on Gene Sullivan's Loyola of Chicago team not getting into any tournaments following 19- and 20-win seasons

"People like me."

Dennis Awtrey, on why he was
traded six times in eight years

"I like to judge a trade by seeing which guys report first."

Bob Ferry, former Bullets GM

"Like they say, there are three things a pro basketball player can't control—injuries, knucklehead coaches, and being traded. Now I can say I've experienced all three."

David Greenwood, after being traded

"When I was with the Sixers, I drank Michelob. In Houston I was forced to switch to Coors and Miller. Now, with the Bulls, I have to start over with Budweiser."

Caldwell Jones, on his tough
adjustment from team to team

"They all wanted to give me bad players, and I've got enough of those."

Stan Kasten, Hawks GM, asked why
he did not make any trades

"I've already lost 220 pounds. We got rid of Dantley. I don't know that much about chemistry, but in terms of physiology, the Dantley trade probably saved my life."

Frank Layden, on trading Adrian
Dantley

"I wish they'd hurry up and find a GM, so I can demand to be traded."

Jawann Oldham, on the Knicks' slow
progress in hiring a GM

"I wouldn't trade Jack Sikma for the resurrection of Marilyn Monroe in my bedroom."

Zollie Volchok, former president of
the Supersonics

"I feel like a fisherman who threw a few worms out there and the fish are laughing at them."

> *Bob Whitsitt, Supersonics president,*
> *after putting every player on the*
> *trading block and making only one*
> *minor deal*

"Obviously, he was a little bit overweight, a little out of shape, but we looked at him and said overweight and out of shape, he's better than anybody we had last year."

> *Tom Wilson, Pistons owner, on*
> *acquiring Oliver Miller*

TRIAL BY JURY

"My life has been a series of trials—but no convictions."

> *Frank Layden*

TRIPLE DOUBLES

"I could use a triple double myself right now."
> *Skip Caray, Hawks announcer, after*
> *Magic Johnson had a triple double*
> *against the Hawks*

"I never knew what a triple double was until last year. I thought they were talking about a horse race."
> *Rick Daly, assistant coach at*
> *Missouri, on one of his players almost*
> *getting a triple double*

"If I would have known it, I would have passed the ball."
> *Karl Malone, on being one assist*
> *short of his first triple double*

"Against Wooden, pretty good. Against Sam Gilbert, not so good."

> *Bob Boyd, former USC coach, asked how he did against John Wooden and UCLA (Sam Gilbert was a prominent UCLA booster)*

"I think Wooden could split his team, send one east, and they'd still end up playing each other in the NCAA final."

> *Digger Phelps, on the great UCLA teams*

UGLY

"No, I was never that ugly."

> *Charles Barkley, asked if Oliver Miller reminded Barkley of himself*

"If the play is confused and fractured, that's good for us. Sometimes the uglier the better. I'm pretty ugly, and we like the team to reflect the coach."

Pete Gillen

"Larry Bird and I might be the two best-looking people from French Lick, Indiana, so that might tell you what kind of ugly rascals they got living in that town."

Jerry Reynolds

ULCERS

"I don't have an ulcer. I'm a carrier. I give them to other people."

Bill Fitch

"To symbolize our great relationship, I'd like you to have this framed x-ray of my ulcer."

Pat Williams, submitting his resignation to 76ers owner Harold Katz

UNDERDOGS

"That's one for the franchise, the team, the coaches, the wives, and our dogs."

>*Don Casey, on the Clippers upsetting one of the great 1980s Lakers teams*

"I think we have a better chance of Our Lady of Fatima reappearing than us beating Purdue."

>*Rick Majerus, on the possibility of Ball State beating Purdue*

"It's a case of the Lions being thrown to the Christians."

>*Wayne Szoke, Columbia University Lions coach, on playing highly ranked St. John's*

UNIFORMS

"I'm just glad to have one."

>*Greg Dreiling, asked to comment on the new ugly uniforms of the Cavaliers*

"Look, they retired Uncle Sam's jersey."

Johnny Kerr, on the American flag flying from the ceiling of Chicago Stadium

"Ugliest things in the league. It's hard to play good when you look so bad."

Dikembe Mutombo, upon hearing the news that the Nuggets were discarding their unattractive uniforms of 1992

"It's almost like a construction worker putting on his tuxedo to go watch Pavarotti."

Robert Reid, on Kurt Rambis in a Hornets designer uniform

"Looking at me in basketball shorts is like looking at Dr. Ruth on the beach in a bikini."

Dick Vitale

"If you're the crème de la crème, you don't send your child to a town where prostitution is practically legal."

> *Elmore Spencer, on UNLV's plans to try to attract a more upscale enrollment*

"If we get one more guy from them, the NBA would probably put us on probation."

> *Reggie Theus, on playing for the Bulls with two other players from UNLV*

"Stacey was a bit disturbed by the salary cap when he came here. They didn't have one at UNLV."

> *Bob Weiss, on signing former UNLV star Stacey Augmon*

"How many times has Bill Walton come back? He's just like Frank Sinatra."

> *Freddie Brown, on another Bill*
> *Walton comeback*

"I told him he may have been the first inductee in history whose speech was longer than his NBA career."

> *Brian McIntyre, NBA VP, on Bill*
> *Walton's 23-minute acceptance speech*
> *upon his induction into the basketball*
> *Hall of Fame*

WAR—WHAT IS IT GOOD FOR?

"The Cubs won, the Jazz were winners, BYU was number one, and if World War III had broken out, Norway would have won."

> *Frank Layden, on 1984, the year of*
> *underdogs*

"When I was 18 years old on my belly in Iwo Jima, I used to comfort myself by thinking, 'Boy, am I lucky not having to deal with the pressure of big-time tennis.'"

Abe Lemons, on John McEnroe complaining about the pressure of being the world's top tennis player

"War is the only game in which it doesn't pay to have the home-court advantage."

Dick Motta

"This year I feel like the U.S. going against Libya. Last year, I felt like Libya."

Mychal Thompson, on being traded from the lowly Spurs to the great Lakers team of Magic and Kareem

"My wife's been on this whole trip. One reason that she and I are still together is that I'm gone a lot. We've been together now for eight straight days, so we might be history."

> *Dick Fick, Morehead State coach, on being stuck in a hotel on the road for several days because of bad weather*

"It's so cold, you'd have to jump-start a reindeer."

> *Mark Herron, Illinois State player, on the cold weather in Illinois*

"I do a lot of the same things—I just do them indoors."

> *Bill Walton, on his lifestyle change after moving to Boston from Los Angeles*

"I got an emergency call from the Edinburg Pizza Hut. They had an all-you-can-eat special for $3.45 and Junior had broken the bank."

> *Dave Brown, assistant coach at Pan American in Edinburg, Texas, on heavyweight Charles "Junior" Ray*

"We all get heavier as we get older, because there's a lot more information in our heads."

> *Vlade Divac, on showing up 15 pounds heavier for training camp*

"He's gotten so fat, he could set a double pick all by himself."

> *Eddie Doucette, on Joe Bryant*

"If we only played like we ate, we'd win this conference."

> *Tommy Joe Eagles, former Auburn coach, on his heavyweight team*

"We look like the number 10."

> *Mike Eisenberg, coach at NYC Technical College, on putting his 5'10", 220-pound frame next to 6'6", 135-pound star player Martin Lacewell*

"Offer him a pizza."

> *Walt Frazier, on the best way to stop the formerly heavy Charles Barkley*

"Last year I felt like I had another person in my shorts."

> *Stacey King, on losing a great deal of weight in the off-season*

"Taking Barkley to 215 would be like asking Raquel Welch to undergo plastic surgery."

> *Bobby Knight, on the college years of Charles Barkley, who weighed 285*

"I happen to have an absolutely beautiful body. The only problem is that it's inside this one."

> *Frank Layden*

"No, but they can put the course around me."
Frank Layden, asked if he would
enter a team marathon

"Scott Williams went from Budweiser to Dom Perignon. So we've got to make sure he gets back on Miller Lite."
John Lucas, on Williams coming to
Philadelphia overweight and with a
big contract

"Rick Majerus losing twenty pounds is like the Queen Mary losing a deck chair."
Al McGuire

"Excellent early conditioning. We take laps around coach Frank Layden."
Calvin Murphy, asked why Niagara
was off to a fast start in 1970

"Last year, Coop was in the doghouse. . . . He's graduated to house pet."
Doug Moe, on Wayne Cooper losing
weight in the off-season

"You can almost run the luge down his stomach."
Billy Packer, on Bobby Knight

"My kitchen became my weight room. I was lifting too many pots and pans."
Glen Rice, on off-season weight problems

"The trade would have been good for him, because restaurants are open later in Detroit."
John Salley, on rumors of the Pistons acquiring the heavyweight Kevin Duckworth for Salley

"If you just eat popcorn and smoke cigars, you wind up losing weight."
Jim Valvano, on his secret for losing weight

"For his 12th birthday, his parents got him a Shetland pony. He carried it out back and barbecued it."
Pat Williams, on Charles Barkley

"Frank went out for baseball, and while he wasn't very good, it wasn't a total loss. The coach used him as a pattern to draw the on-deck circle."
Pat Williams, on Frank Layden

WILT THE STILT

"I don't say Wilt Chamberlain is the strongest man I've ever known, but when he wipes the sweat off his brow, people in the balcony get a bath."
Bill Fitch

WINNING

"Winning is overrated. The only time it is really important is in surgery and war."
Al McGuire

"They used to call me nuts, but when we started winning, they called me eccentric. The only difference between being eccentric and being nuts is the number of security boxes you own."
Al McGuire

"Once you start keeping score, winning's the bottom line. It's the American concept. If not, it's like your grandmother, and even then you try to win unless she has a lot of money and you want to get some of it."

Al McGuire

"If I've got to pass out to win every game, it's going to be hard."

Jerry Reynolds, on being rushed to the hospital during a game the Kings eventually won

"There's only two things in the NBA. There's winning and there's misery."

Pat Riley

"Very simple. Nothing will work unless you do."

John Wooden, on the secret of winning

"The athlete who says that something cannot be done should never interrupt the one who is doing it."

John Wooden

WOMEN'S BASKETBALL LEAGUE

"The WBL is great. It gives women like me who don't want to work something to do."
Linnell Jones

JOHN WOODEN

"John Wooden was so square, he was divisible by four."
Jim Murray

WORKING STIFF

"Yeah, I get paid to do it, too."
Scott Hastings, on being called a stiff by a fan

"Am I eligible for unemployment?"
John Johnson, on being released after 12 seasons with the Supersonics

"If I were reincarnated, I'd want to come back with rich parents. I'd buy me a yacht and go off to the Caribbean to watch the ocean turn from brown to blue. I'm not crazy about working hard."

Abe Lemons, asked if he would be a basketball coach if he were reincarnated

"He said he'd given his employers 30 of the best years of his life. Now he'd give them a few of the bad ones."

Bill Russell, on why his father would not retire

"There are two kinds of people in the world, the ones who do the work and the ones who want to take credit for doing the work. You're better off in the first group—there's a lot less competition."

Kelvin Sampson, Oklahoma coach

"We have black players, white players, a Mormon, and four Yugoslavians. Our toughest decision isn't what offense or defense to run, but what type of warm-up music to play."

Tim Capstraw, Wagner coach

"Don't you think there is some rich Arab out there who'd pay to have his kid on the Knicks?"

Frank Layden, on his plan to increase rosters to 15 and have 6 players on each team pay for playing on the team

"I can't remember the names of all the clubs we went to."

Shaquille O'Neal, on being asked if he saw the Parthenon when he was in Greece

"I hope they don't let Charles Barkley get a taste of our German beer. If he gets into that, we could have a problem."

Detlef Schrempf, on the Phoenix Suns touring Germany

"He kept saying what a great hotel we were in. Then came the last day—he complained the towels were so thick he couldn't close his suitcase."

Jim Valvano, after being on a
European tour with Rollie Massimino

"I didn't know the pope shopped."

Jim Valvano, on being told that the
pope shopped in the same luggage
store in Florence, Italy, that Valvano
was in

THE WORM

"You go beyond the hair, tattoos, and the earrings, and he's like you and I."

Bob Hill, on Dennis Rodman

"Whatever he's doing gets him 18 rebounds a game. I might have to paint my hair orange. He might be the normal one and all of us might be crazy. Ever think of that?"

Malik Sealy, on Dennis Rodman

INDEX